D0721009

FINDING TIME TO LEAD

*Seven Practices to Unleash
Outrageous Potential*

BY LESLIE PETERS

ADVANCE PRAISE

"Finding Time to Lead compels us to explore the intersection of what it means to *be a leader* and to *be human.* Leslie Peters brings a no bullshit, straight-talk perspective to the unique responsibility of leadership— with compelling real-life stories and a clear pathway to guide the very human leader inside us all."

DEAN CARTER
Head of Finance, HR and Legal at Patagonia

"Practical and inspirational, *Finding Time to Lead* is an essential field guide for any leader who seeks to be both successful *and* truly human."

SARA HANNAH
Managing Partner at BW Leadership Institute

"Finding Time to Lead is accessible and still profoundly connected to the deeper concepts in leadership theory. This book is a practical guide that will be very helpful to all managers, not just CEOs, who wish to practice the art of leadership."

PAUL EICHEN
Founder and CEO of Rokenbok Education

"Leslie Peters has produced an engaging and helpful guide to making the shifts necessary to successfully manage a top leadership role, with all of the complexity and uncertainty this entails."

LUCY ENGLISH
PhD, Managing Director of Institutional Research at Bright Horizons

---

"In *Finding Time to Lead*, Leslie Peters establishes herself as an essential voice for the kind of aspirational leadership that builds great, sustainable companies. The practices and tools in this book are sure to accelerate your journey toward becoming the leader you want to be."

STUART KERR
SVP of Global Enterprise Business at Fleetmatics (A Verizon Company)

"Leslie Peters draws upon readings, conversations, and experiences and puts them together in a powerful way that informs and inspires. She shows us how to learn from observing others and from reflecting on our own behaviors. Every reader will benefit from her insights and pragmatic approach to leadership and growth."

THOMAS R. HOERR, PHD
Emeritus Head of New City School, and Founder of the Nonprofit Management Program at Washington University

---

"Leslie Peters provides practical tools for people who are passionate about becoming the kind of leader they aspire to be—no matter where they are on the org. chart. Make time to read this book! You'll be glad you did."

JOHN LIPSEY
VP of Corporate Communications at Flexera Software

COPYRIGHT

Cover Design: Doreen Hann

Editing: Grace Kerina

Author's photo courtesy of Lillian Peters

DEDICATION

For Dan, whose presence in my life has changed everything.

TABLE OF CONTENTS

FOREWORD

Before I had ever contemplated the idea of a personal leadership approach, I had gotten my MBA, read all of the must-read business books, and built a successful career developing new products and playing key roles in a significantly growing business. I had a bias for moving fast. I took cues from leaders whose charisma and instincts seemed larger than life and innate.

When I then became the CEO of a subsidiary of a large bank, I knew the job was big, that I had much to learn, and that I would need to show up differently than I had before. I wondered what characteristics of my prior bosses I could borrow or steal. How might I ask questions like this person, or communicate like that one? If I bolted enough pieces together, could I fool everyone and look like a leader? I spent a good deal of time trying.

Then, a few years ago, we had the opportunity to grow our business significantly over a short period of time. I knew that we had high-performing and talented people in our company. I knew that to get where we wanted to go we would have to significantly broaden our enterprise level leadership and rapidly accelerate their capacity to lead. And I knew that, at that moment, I didn't have all of the personal experience or capacity to get us there.

Enter Leslie Peters. When I engaged Leslie and her firm, Elements Partnership, to coordinate an all-company meeting, I had no inkling that she would, over time, thoughtfully draw open a curtain and allow me to see something absolutely critical and life-changing: that with care and practice, with awareness and attention, by doing the work to know myself and listen well to others, the most vital and dynamic leader I could ever hope to be was *me*.

There would be no bolting pieces stolen from others, but there would instead be time spent recognizing who I am and where I come from. I would come to know the influences that brought me to certain places at certain points in time, and I began to see how my experiences had created my view and vision of the world. I came to appreciate the stories and narratives I have about how that world works and how those stories and narratives influence me... sometimes for the better and sometimes not.

This knowledge has become the platform from which my personal leadership practice has emerged. This recognition has given me the insight to work at being present. I actively seek to be seen and heard as I intend. It's never perfect, but I try to do things *on* purpose, and *with* purpose. I think about leadership as someone I am, not just something I do.

By demystifying the most crucial components of leadership, and putting words to them, Leslie offers the tools to practice leadership with humility and confidence at the same time. She demonstrates the liberating value of knowing and stating our own assets and limitations. The perspectives and practices in *Finding Time to Lead* give us the power to show up with the clarity to lead.

In my experience, shared by others at my company, exercising these muscles not only leads us to perform more effectively at work, but it also enriches us personally. Leslie's approach to leadership artfully weaves together the personal and the professional, which makes it more than a passing fad or something we do because it will help us get ahead in our careers. In my organization, we have adopted this approach because it makes a meaningful difference in our lives.

I participated in one of the Elements Partnership leadership programs, not as the CEO, but as a peer to my other 12 colleagues, members of my staff representing various levels in our organizational hierarchy, none of whom reported directly to me. Over the course of the program, what emerged among all of us was a poignant gratitude, not only for the tools being learned, but for the space provided for us to explore matters of leadership, the "call" to step into it, the path that unfolds.

Amidst the frenetic pace of the everyday, some anticipated they would be distracted and unable to focus. In fact, the opposite occurred. We came to know ourselves and one another more deeply. We were able to be individuals, not on stage, performing a role, but in three dimensions, with a history, a story, imperfections, strengths and aspirations. We saw the way that a commitment to empathy, honesty and courage could build a sweeping energy, a supportive space and forward motion.

The commitment to these principles has built for us an extremely strong foundation, an environment that, while ever evolving and improving, is characterized by honest reflection, authentic engagement, acknowledgment of individual limitations, identification of individual and organizational strengths, courageous conversations and rich interpersonal connections built on trust.

In action, this looks like a group that shares clarity of purpose and people leveraging their strengths for the good of the whole. It creates opportunity for incisive communication, accelerated problem solving, and collaborative execution. Utilizing many of the concepts and tools described in *Finding Time to Lead*, we are building a culture of embedded leadership - leadership at every level - that I believe will be a defining feature of our future success.

The work of leadership is messy in its many dimensions. Leslie inspires us to relish these layers, exploring complexity, not with the intent to master, but to seek the discomfort at the edges—constantly growing and improving so that we might push forward to the next edge. We want to stretch and reach past who we are today, to push the edge to find out who we can be. These are the things that move an organization forward.

At Leslie's suggestion, I sent a note to myself a few months ago and it arrived recently. This is what I reminded myself: *"Believe that you know the right thing to do—then say it and do it. Make sure you're taking the time to THINK, LISTEN and REFLECT. Tackle the hard issues. Don't wait. Make sure we're reaching to be better."*

My business has grown significantly since Leslie Peters arrived on the scene, and it has been a profound pleasure to live the moments of shared success with her. Today, my organization is taking on new tests and addressing far more complex demands than ever, both within our own organization and in our broader industry. Even more, we are inspired to leverage who we are and what we do to make deeper and lasting impacts on some of the most difficult challenges in our society. In my view, we are well positioned for this work, the next chapter in our organization's story, in large part because of our commitment to the tenets found in *Finding Time to Lead*.

We have the courage to believe we can succeed, because we understand that it is people and these practices that can take us there. With humility, we can decide how we will show up and take it on. We are embracing the future with honesty, empathy, courage and curiosity.

To lead is a privilege, a great responsibility and a special opportunity. Much like other privileges, we can too often take our role as leaders for granted, forgotten, like the air we breathe. We can drive hard and stay busy, filling our schedules. We can measure production and report on results. We can be subject matter experts and look the part.

When we forget that leadership is privilege, a great responsibility and a special opportunity, we fail to tend to it, examine it, and cultivate it. We fail to find time for it. Leslie Peters asks more of us.

Finding Time to Lead lays out a path for leaders at every level to understand what true leadership means, what it looks like to practice it with intention, and how that practice can develop within each of us the capacity to stretch, create and have a lasting impact on the people we serve—in our organizations, our communities and our families. We do not take our privilege, our leadership, for granted. We choose to tend to it, to practice it, and to commit to it. The line is almost never straight, but the direction is known.

With Leslie's partnership, we are building a business of leaders, an inspired organization with aspirations to be ever greater by harnessing the power of an approach that values thoughtfulness and deliberateness, that prioritizes learning and listening, engaging and reflecting, and that prefers mentors to heroes.

I am grateful for the opportunity to speak to and validate the value of Leslie's counsel and approach. *Finding Time to Lead* is a thoughtful and joyful reflection of her wisdom. It provides a valuable set of learnings and reminders that have made a critical difference for me and that I believe will make a real difference for you. Enjoy.

ZACHARY M. BOYERS
Chairman & C.E.O.
U.S. Bancorp Community Development Corporation

INTRODUCTION

"After all has been said and done, what we have to offer is our authentic selves in relationship to others. What matters most, what transforms, is the influence of a humble, vulnerable witness to the truth."

~ Henri Nouwen

THERE IS NO CEO SCHOOL

There is no specific school or program people can attend to learn to be a CEO. There is just too much to know.

Where does "leadership" fit into all of the million other things you need to know and do? How do you make time for "leadership"? If you had the time for it, how would you spend that time?

I've spent the last 20-plus years working side by side with CEOs. I've served as a consultant, coach, trainer, second in command, confidante, and friend to CEOs at all different kinds of organizations, and I am now the CEO of my own small company. Some of the people I've known in the CEO role have had extraordinary careers. They've built incredible cultures, grown their companies, enhanced the bottom line, and left a meaningful and positive mark on organizations they care about.

I've also known CEOs who have burned out, caused the culture in their organizations to stagnate, and led their organizations into ruin.

Generally, we promote people to be CEO because they're extraordinarily good at something the organization cares about—sales and marketing, product development, or engineering. In a start-up, it's the person with a great idea for a new product or service who becomes the CEO, because they had the great idea. In nonprofit organizations, we promote our best teachers to be principals and our best social workers to be executive directors.

When we do that, we put extraordinarily talented, high-achieving people into a role that is entirely new to them. We ask them to do something totally different than any-thing they've done before. We pull them away from the thing in which they've excelled. It's like pulling the star center off the varsity basketball team and asking him to coach the soccer team.

The role of CEO requires a very different skill set than any other company role. The view of the organization, the span of control and authority, and the level of responsibility and pressure are all different from the CEO's chair. It's excit-ing and exhilarating, but also overwhelming. CEOs—espe-cially new CEOs—learn on the job, all the time... and the stakes are high.

Of course, every CEO comes into their new role with great aspirations about the type of incredible leader they'll be.

They want to be like their favorite coach or mentor. And then they get sucked into the minutiae of the job and put "leadership" on the back burner. Or, worse yet, they equate doing things and making decisions with leadership, which is not to say that those aren't components of leadership, but they are not the most important part of a CEO's job.

Condensing leadership into "doing things and making decisions" lets us off the hook from considering a broader definition of leadership.

Our beliefs are where we begin. The decisions we make and the things we do merely reinforce what we believe. *Intentionally choosing* what we will do and how we show up is where leadership lives.

How do you intentionally choose? Especially when there is so much to do and there are so many decisions to make? Intentional choice depends on knowing what you care about. So, what do you care about? And how might you find time to figure that out?

The good news is that it doesn't take all that much time. It takes *focused* time on things that matter the most. That's what this book is about. I'll show you three shifts, seven practices, and lots of tools that will help you learn how to be a CEO, or a leader at any level.

As it turns out, it's not hard to find time to lead, because leading is already inherent in *everything* you do. It's not something separate that you have to *make* time for.

I've seen CEOs who take a lifetime to feel like they've got the perspective and platform in their own leadership to do what they want to do with their company. I've seen CEOs who never get there. And I've seen CEOs who are hungry, who are eager to embrace their new role, who see themselves growing and extending to unleash their own greatness and the greatness in their people.

Which one are you?

I'm assuming, since you picked up this book, that you're a hungry CEO, that you want to accelerate your own path to great leadership. You're ready for clarity about where you should be spending your limited time and how to spend it in a way that will expand your leadership capacity. This book will challenge you to do some real work on learning how to be a CEO, because there's greatness in you. Others have seen it. You've experienced it. Let's make sure it gets out there—all the time.

In this book, I'll begin with three fundamental shifts that broaden the view of leadership and demonstrate how it is embedded in everything you already do. These shifts are adapted from the work of my friend and colleague Kimberly Schneider, MEd, JD, LPC, who teaches Communication and Presence to university students and business leaders. Within each of these shifts, we'll look at two supportive practices, along with specific tools you can use right now. We'll wrap up with a seventh practice that is the foundation for all the others.

The shifts, practices, and tools in *Finding Time to Lead* will give you the perspectives you need to tap into the powerful base that is your own personal leadership. You'll have what you need to be the type of leader who can engage with others to build a culture that attracts and keeps incredible people, that innovates, and that adapts and maximizes the opportunities available to create the future you imagine— not only for your company, but for yourself.

WHY "SHIFT"?

Shifting a perspective or a stance is like adjusting the lens on a camera. Imagine taking a photograph with your phone. You can see only what's in the boundary of the camera's lens. You can zoom in and get closer to the details, but you can't get a broader view than what's allowed by the frame.

Now imagine physically turning the camera to "panorama" view. Your perspective shifts. That's what these CEO shifts will do for you—they'll expand your view.

When you're able to see more, you're able to *choose* better about what to pay attention to. With that expanded view, you can step back and see more and different options. And you can make more conscious choices.

Here's the big secret about leadership and why you don't have to *make* time for it: *It's not a separate thing*. It is part of everything you already do.

Making these perspective shifts will simply and radically change what you're *already doing*.

THE THREE SHIFTS

Remember how great you were at your last job? Remember that incredible idea that prompted you to start your company? It's a fantastic feeling! You were on top of the world, excited about what you'd accomplished and ready for the next challenge, or eager to be the greatest tech company or new product on the market.

Then you sit in the CEO's chair and realize that this job is *big*. It's exciting and full of opportunity and *big*. Everyone is looking at you expecting you to *lead*. What does that mean? What does it mean for you?

In my experience, great leaders have gone through three big shifts in perspective and action. If you can understand these shifts and begin to integrate them into how you operate as a leader, you can vastly accelerate your own journey toward great leadership.

The three big shifts that happen for great leaders are:

- From doing to being
- From knowing to understanding
- From reacting to responding

One of the challenging things about these shifts is that they're not only shifts; they're *expansions*. As a CEO, you will be called to do, know, and react, but, more often, you will find yourself needing to be, understand, and respond. The trick is figuring out which one in what measure and in what circumstances.

I'll give you seven practices and more than twenty tools that you can start using immediately to accelerate these shifts and expand your capacity as a leader. But first let's briefly explore each of these shifts in a bit more depth.

THE FIRST SHIFT:
FROM DOING TO BEING

As a CEO, of course you *do* things. There are many things to *do*, but you've probably noticed that you're not as productive as you used to be. Being a great leader is a *looong* game. There are fewer check-it-off-the-list things to accomplish, fewer things you can say are done, and very few actions you take that don't then have multiple next steps in terms of communicating and building alignment.

It can be frustrating to not have that one big goal: "I met the sales goals for this quarter!" "I completed that prototype on deadline!" "I kept that project on budget!" "I got the next round of funding!" It's great when those goals are met, but as CEO you see the other seventeen goals that aren't being met and your attention goes there.

The issues you address and the problems you see are long-term, slow, simmering problems that require time for answers and solutions to emerge. Organizations are complex systems and *doing* things in the moment isn't usually the answer in a complex system. Sitting with the discomfort of not knowing is more often the answer, because it allows a better view of the whole. This means that you have to *be* in that space of allowing a wider perspective, not necessarily *doing* something right now.

This move from doing to being is the most impactful and most challenging shift. You've probably always been aware of who you are, and I'm sure you've paid attention to how you show up—how you behave and interact in different situations. You wouldn't be the CEO if you hadn't. But this role of CEO is different. Everything you do is at an exponentially higher level. The stakes are higher.

Chapters 1 and 2 explore the two practices—*Embark* and *Explore*—that provide the foundation for moving from *doing* to *being*.

THE SECOND SHIFT:
FROM KNOWING TO UNDERSTANDING

It's great to *know*, isn't it? To have the answer, to see that end-game, to be able to add up the numbers and be sure of the results. We like that. Our brains are wired for it. As high-achieving, successful people we *really* like that—*especially* when we're the ones who know.

Certainty is comfortable for the most primitive, unconscious, and, in some ways, most powerful, part of our brain, the part that generates chemicals that trigger our fight-or-flight response. This part of the brain developed back in the days when we had to be wary of predators. It kept us alive and allowed us to survive as a species. If things are certain, this most primitive part of our brain doesn't have to be scanning for danger all the time. It can relax. We feel better.

Because of this, we pursue certainty like a heat-seeking missile. Often to our detriment.

When we *know*, we are in that zone of certainty where we feel most comfortable. We think we've solved something and we literally breathe a sigh of relief. We often look to leaders to provide that certainty, to make us feel more comfortable. As a leader, there are certainly times to offer comfort, but certainty is an illusion. More often than not, rather than provide "the answers," our most important job as CEO is to help people feel more safe in their discomfort.

Winston Churchill is a good example of this shift from knowing to understanding. He couldn't *know* the outcome of World War II. There were no clear answers. No one could *know*. And there wasn't much he could *do* from his underground bunker in London. But he understood that people were frightened. He comprehended the complexity of the situation and he was able to *be* a leader. What he said, how he showed up, how he demonstrated that understanding was all he could do, because he could not know. The way he handled *not* knowing made him a leader for that time.

In uncertain times—which are really pretty much all times—understanding and holding space for *not* knowing may be our best contribution as leaders.

Chapters 3 and 4 explore two practices—*Expand* and *Engage*—that support the shift from knowing to understanding. In those chapters, you'll also find frameworks and approaches to help you move more quickly from knowing to understanding.

THE THIRD SHIFT:
FROM REACTING TO RESPONDING

We prize quick reactions, especially in fast-paced environments like today's companies and start-ups. "You snooze; you lose," is a story we tell ourselves to justify quick reactions. We look for people who can give us a quick answer so that we can keep things moving.

There's a place for that, but it's generally not in the CEO's office.

Responding instead of reacting does not mean moving slowly. It means incorporating thought and foresight in your response. *Responding* comes from being, not doing. It reflects understanding, which may include *not* knowing (at least not in this moment).

I have a client who is a very young, very brilliant CEO of a start-up tech company. When he was starting his venture, he got advice and counsel from lots of people, including investors, professors, and fellow entrepreneurs. As we talked about leadership, he reflected on all the questions those people *didn't* ask him about starting a company and taking on the role of CEO. "People ask you about your market share and your capitalization and your time to prototype," he said. "But they don't ask you about how you see yourself as a leader. No one asked me the kinds of questions that would have given me insight into the role of the CEO or how I would fill that role."

I asked him if he could identify some things that might have turned out differently if he'd had conversations beforehand about the role of CEO. He could immediately point to one exact moment that would have changed the trajectory of his company.

He was in a dispute with his founding partner and they were in negotiations about how to unwind their partnership. There had been a bit of lawyering, and the negotiations had gotten tense, but not acrimonious. The partner called to offer a potential settlement deal, the terms of which were outside of what my client had considered, and he blew up. "Hell, no! We're not doing that."

From that point on, the negotiations became acrimonious, dragging out for months. The settlement deal he later faced was not nearly as favorable as the terms that were given in that phone call offering the potential settlement deal. Because of that, the future of his company is in jeopardy and the great idea that inspired him to start his company may never see the light of day. He identifies *that moment* as the turning point and realizes that his actions in that moment put his company on this path.

"If I had known then how important it is to just stop and think... if I had been trained to *respond* instead of *react*, I might have recognized that the terms he was offering were not unreasonable, even though they were outside of what I had considered up to that point. I would have known that I needed to give myself time to expand my thinking so that I could respond more effectively. Instead, I reacted in the moment and blew the deal."

That's perhaps an extreme example, but I'll bet you can think of situations where your reaction set in motion a series of events that ended up being, at best, counter-productive and, at worst, destructive. (Did you just raise your eyebrows and nod your head?) We've all been there.

The bottom line is that, as a CEO, you can't afford to react instead of respond.

Your actions carry tremendous weight. The ability to *respond*—to people, situations, and decisions—in a way that is thoughtful and that leverages your broad view and best thinking, is critical for making the most of the opportunities available to you in this role and to your company.

The capacity to respond instead of only react is one of the key things that enables you to intentionally create a culture that attracts and keeps the best people. More importantly, it's what maximizes their potential, because it generates commitment and loyalty.

Chapters 5 and 6 focus on the shift from reacting to responding and explores how this shift unleashes the potential in your people, through two practices—*Encourage* and *Evolve*.

Chapter 7 is about the final practice, *Extend*. This practice is a simple reminder you can use when you feel like you can't possibly find enough time to be bothered with all of this "leadership stuff."

ONE MORE THING

Just one more note before you go on. We're all achievement-oriented, results-driven, successful people here, and we like to get things *done*. Therefore, it's only fair to warn you that making these shifts is never *done*. This is a practice—and it takes *lots* of practice.

If you're looking for a silver bullet or a magic pill that will suddenly transform you into the great leader you want to be (if you're not up for doing the work of learning to be a great leader), then this book is not for you.

Being a leader and learning how to be a better leader is not for the faint of heart. If you really want it... keep reading.

PART ONE

– THE FIRST SHIFT –
FROM DOING TO BEING

Doing to being is the first and most impactful shift. The other two shifts don't happen unless this shift happens first.

The two practices that help you move from doing to being are *Embark* and *Explore*, which we'll explore in the next two chapters.

CHAPTER 1

EMBARK

You know that moment when you cross the threshold from the Jetway into the airplane? The air changes and you have that sense of anticipation (or dread) about the flight and about the work or play that awaits you on your journey. You might wonder how the experience will play out. Will you get the client? Will the meeting go well? Will you still like your spouse/partner/kids after this vacation?

Whether you consciously stop to consider it or not, you will be changed by this experience. The change might be subtle or it might be big, but you will carry it with you and there will be no going back.

There is a moment when you *choose* to take that step onto the airplane or settle in behind the wheel of your car, a moment when you consciously decide to *Embark* on that journey. Even if you've been to the destination a thousand times, you're still setting off into the unknown.

This is that moment for you as a CEO. Will you choose to *Embark* on this journey toward being the kind of leader you aspire to be? Or will you convince yourself that you don't really have time for all that "leadership stuff?"

You can shrink-wrap your leadership into the small box of *getting things done* (lots of successful people do). You can continue to do things that will *prove* you're worthy of this position and that you know how to lead. *Or* you can challenge yourself to let go of the things that made you extraordinary before; you can be humble in the face of the vast learning required for this role and recognize that *being*—showing up as your best possible self—is now what you *do.*

This is when you physically shift the lens from showing a small photo frame to showing a panoramic view.

Are you up for that?

This is not a journey of arriving quickly at a pre-determined destination. This is about choosing a path and accelerating on that path by knowing where to put your attention.

By making these shifts, integrating the practices in this book, and using these tools, you will find time to lead—not because you suddenly have more time, but because you will understand that leading is a natural part of everything you do. You will no longer think you have to *make* time for leadership. Leadership simply becomes the operating system for every action, decision, and interaction you have.

But, first, you have to take that conscious step, make that choice, to *Embark* on the journey.

YEP, THIS IS DIFFERENT

You've probably already had a feeling that being a CEO is very different. You're no longer as busy doing things—managing projects, working out the details of a plan, or building sales and marketing strategies. Maybe you've actually said out loud, "I don't feel like I really do anything anymore." You may be asking yourself if everyone around you is wondering what you do and what value you add.

In a training session I did with new managers, one person shared what they were all thinking: "If I don't do the job I was doing, then what's my value? I don't understand."

The head of human resources for a large academic/medical institution shared with me the challenges of asking professors and doctors to shift their time and attention from their specific area of expertise to leading and managing people. "These people are national leaders in their field. Why would they *want* to spend their time doing anything but focusing on the areas in which they've built their expertise?"

And then there's the role of CEO, which is different still. For a CEO, everything operates at a different level. Even meetings with people are less about the actual doing. Your conversations have probably shifted from, "How are we going to solve this software glitch?" to questions like, "How do we get our software engineers to feel ownership for meeting customers' needs?"

The things you talk about and think about as a CEO are bigger and more complex than you've faced before, and your level of responsibility and control are greater. The questions that occupy a CEO's thoughts don't have easy or immediate answers; the problems don't have easy or immediate solutions.

Once you've chosen to *Embark* on this journey, the next step is to understand more about how the landscape changes from the vantage point of the CEO's chair.

ACKNOWLEDGING COMPLEXITY

Today's organizations are incredibly complex. What used to exist in buildings and factories and fields now exists in networks of people and in and among other complex systems. Products exist in people's heads—at least initially, and sometimes solely. We no longer measure the vast portion of our commerce in tangible 3-D things that can be built, counted, and shipped.

This makes the work of leadership and measuring success exponentially more challenging. Humans are a bigger part of the equation than ever and, let's face it, anytime you add human beings to an equation, things get messy.

Compare answering the question, "How do we build a bridge over this river?" to "How do we get our software engineers to feel ownership for meeting customer needs?".

Building a bridge over a river is a *complicated* problem. Granted, it's a very complicated problem, but there is an answer. We study the river and the embankments. We hire experts. We learn from comparable past experiences with other bridges. Data is useful and past experience can fairly directly inform our current problem. That's how solutions work when it's a complicated problem. We certainly have some of those kinds of problems in our organizations.

More often, though, especially from the CEO's chair, the problems we face are not only complicated, they are *complex*. There aren't experts you can hire who will have the answer for your particular problem in your particular company. Past experience may or may not accurately inform the current situation. And, if there *is* data, the data you have today may not be relevant tomorrow.

"How do we get our engineers to feel ownership for meeting customer needs?" is not a problem to solve and move on from. Those engineers and the software they develop and the customers who use it are all parts of a larger complex system *that is never static*.

The start-up that has five employees, the non-profit daycare center, the company with 100 or 1,000 employees—are all complex, ever-changing systems. And everything is made even more complex when the organization is growing.

In complex systems, answers don't readily appear; they *emerge*. This creates a great deal of uncertainty. We humans don't like uncertainty. Our brains are hard-wired to avoid it. We prefer a bad certainty to a good *un*certainty. We can't even really imagine a *good* uncertainty.

And yet, in complex systems, if the answer is to emerge, there *must* be a space between identifying a problem or asking a hard question and the emergence of that answer or solution. It is in that space that we feel uncertainty.

Choosing to *Embark* on this journey requires us to acknowledge the complexity inherent in any gathering of human beings. The shifts and practices in this book give us the opportunity to acknowledge uncertainty—and choose it anyway. Pursuing this path of great leadership enables us to step into uncertainty that can feel like chaos, even though our brains believe chaos is something to be avoided at all cost.

Chaos looks crazy and unpredictable and dangerous, but uncertainty, even when it feels like chaos, does not mean that there is no order. In her book *Leadership and the New Science*, Margaret Wheatley describes chaos as "order without predictability." There *is* inherent order in complex systems, although they may lack the predictability that makes us comfortable.

COMPLEXITY IN ACTION

Complex systems are inherently unpredictable. Leading in this kind of complexity and uncertainty requires a different set of skills and perspectives that are leveraged from an entirely different point of view. We can't *Embark* on the path toward great leadership without accepting this reality.

As an example, I serve on the board of directors of a charter school that is committed to dismantling the systems of racism and poverty that plague our city and our country, which is a *very* complicated problem.

As the school has evolved, it has been in what feels like a constant state of chaos. Teachers and administrators—some beloved and some reviled—have come and gone. The parent community has been challenged and challenging. We've had people try to entice us to replicate, and we've had people try to shut us down.

And now, as we've tried things and failed, tried things and succeeded, created systems, gotten clear about our principles and what we care about, and held firm to those principles in the face of very real threats, we are able to see patterns—we can identify the things that got us off track and the things that are required to keep us on track. We recognize threats and opportunities with new eyes and with a shared understanding of what they mean.

For example, a few years ago, we moved into a new building, which was a huge step that prompted remarkable reinvestment in our neighborhood. And... that investment now threatens the very diversity that the school was founded to address because housing prices have increased to the point that the socio-economic diversity is threatened.

Every step into new territory, each step forward, brings new challenges. Nothing about this journey has been, or will be, predictable. (Believe me I can tell you stories.) But we have steadily trained ourselves to see the patterns to the best of our abilities. We understand that there is order in what appears to be chaos and we look for the patterns that will reveal where our actions are paying off and where they're not, so that we can make meaningful adjustments that might have an impact on the things we care about.

This is *not* easy. In my experiences with CEOs, including the CEO of this school, I've seen how hard it is to lead in uncertainty. It requires a completely new set of skills, a different kind of awareness, and an ability to be patient as things emerge.

What makes it especially challenging to lead in uncertainty is that we humans *especially* hate uncertainty in high-achieving, successful cultures. We want answers. We want to solve this *now*. We want to be told what to do to resolve this issue—or we want to make the decision about what to do ourselves—so that we can move on to the next thing.

However, it is in this gap, in this constant uncertainty, in the chaos necessary for patterns to reveal themselves, that solutions emerge. And this is where great leaders show up. Not to *do* anything, but to *be* present—to walk with, beside, in front of, and sometimes behind, the people who find themselves in the inevitable uncertainty of complex systems.

We can't lead this way unless we make the choice to embrace the uncertainty of where our own journey will take us, unless we *Embark* consciously on our own personal leadership journey.

THE CEO SECRET FOR *EMBARK*

Being a leader is not something you *do*; it's someone you *are*. You have the power to *choose* who you want to *be*.

TOOL 1:
EMBARK ON THE JOURNEY

Making the shift from doing to being, from knowing to understanding, and from reacting to responding is not something you *do*, it is a path you are on. It's a journey toward a destination that is constantly moving.

Some days, the path will be clear and you'll make great progress and feel good about how far you've come. Some days you'll feel like you've gone in a big circle and ended up back where you started.

Being on this journey requires a *decision* to embark, a moment when we consciously choose to shift the lens, when we settle in behind the wheel and contemplate what's ahead, knowing that we can't predict how it might change us.

Peter Block, author of *The Answer to How is Yes,* describes taking responsibility for ourselves this way: "My freedom, my purpose, my learning, are all faces of the same intention: living out my own destiny and bringing this into the world with all the worth and generosity I can muster."

This is a basic tool: Recognize that leadership is a journey and make the decision to *Embark*.

TOOL 2:
ASK YOURSELF, "WHO DO I WANT TO BE RIGHT NOW?"

Asking yourself, "Who do I want to be right now?" is a quick and reliable way of giving yourself choices about how you want to show up in any given moment.

I was in a meeting recently and one of the leaders of the organization came in and sat down next to me. She said, "All day today I've been hearing you in my head telling me to ask myself 'Who do I want to be right now?'" Her division's goal was increased from $250M to $400M this year and they are *crazed*. She is an incredible expert and her default mode is to give people quick answers, so that everyone can keep moving at breakneck speed. She recently realized that that's not helping her team in the long run. Even with this huge new goal, she needs to invest in the long-term by supporting people in coming to their own solutions.

This day was particularly stressful, and she was feeling an incredible pull to revert to her default mode of *doing*—of giving answers and solving problems for people, but she's made the first shift. She knows that, in her role, *being* is more important than *doing*. Asking herself, "Who do I want to be right now?" was a powerful way to pull back from the situation and make more conscious choices.

"Who do I want to be right now?" is a very different question than, "What do I want to do right now?"

So, who *do* you want to be right now?

Think of someone you admire a great deal. They could be a teacher, parent, spouse, or friend, a boss or colleague, a fictional character, or a figure from history. Think of a number of people you admire. What is it that you admire about them? What is it about them that you would *desperately* like to be able to display in your own interactions with people?

Build a repertoire of people you want to emulate (your dad, mom, favorite boss, coach, teacher, character from literature or film). When you find yourself in a stressful situation (or every morning as you start your day) ask yourself, "Who do I want to be right now?" Those people will show up with all of their great qualities. Choose one. Be *that* person as you step forward into the situations and circumstances that might challenge you—not the person who wants to tell someone to quit their whining and get back to work.

Asking yourself "Who do I want to be right now?" is a way of expanding your expectations of yourself, of setting an aspirational goal for how you'll show up, and then being able to *choose* to show up that way.

The question of this tool is a reminder that a CEO (a leader of any kind) is someone you *are*, not something you *do*.

For me, the person I most want to be like is my friend Jim McLeod. Jim was an associate chancellor at the university I attended and he was a friend of mine for many years until he died of cancer at the age of 67. All of us who knew Jim (and there were thousands over his 30-plus years at the university) have "Jim-isms" that we refer to regularly. My personal favorite is *"All greatness comes from goodness."* It's posted on the bulletin board above my desk.

At Jim's memorial service, a colleague of his described walking across campus with Jim. He talked about how it would take *forever*. (Jim was late to every meeting.) It would take so long because Jim was like the shepherd who was always scanning for lost sheep. He would spy the student sitting on the steps by herself, or the group of African-American students gathered at the corner of the library, or the family on a tour who looked like they might be lost. Jim would notice them and then reach out to them—every time.

When I'm feeling like I have to quickly get to my next meeting, or get done whatever has to get done right now, and I notice a particular issue or person that I know is important I ask myself, "Who do I want to be right now?" Very often Jim pops into my head. I think of Jim and the story of him being like a shepherd. I remember that "all greatness comes from goodness," and I choose to slow down and show up exactly as I want to be in that moment.

And the best part? It takes barely seconds and it often saves a lot of time later.

(You can find the full list of these questions in worksheet form on our website: FindingTimeToLead.com. Throughout the book, you'll see references to FindingTimeToLead.com where you'll find a wide range of free resources, links, downloadable files, worksheets, audio files, and more.)

TOOL 3:
LISTEN ON THREE LEVELS

One of the most observable traits of a leader who has made the shift from doing to being is that they listen more than they talk. And they don't just listen; they listen *well.*

Let's look at three levels of listening: faux, focused and epic. Each is good in its own way.

Level 1—Faux Listening. The first, and most common, level of listening is faux listening. This is when we look like we're listening (we might even be leaning in and nodding—things we're taught to do to demonstrate that we're listening) but, in our heads, we're thinking about what we'll say or about a story that relates to what the speaker is saying or a witty or insightful comment we can make about the speaker's story or issue.

In that moment when we're thinking about our story, we're thinking about ourselves and how we appear to others. We're *not* listening to what the other person is saying.

Sometimes faux listening is fine. Talking about where we'll go for lunch or when we'll have that meeting or how we feel about a particular sports team or movie—those are topics that benefit from the give and take of stories and associations. Sometimes, though, it's not enough.

Level 2—Focused Listening. When someone is talking to us about the importance of a project or a particular situation on their team, a different kind of listening is useful: focused listening. Focused listening is when you really focus on the words someone is saying. You're really taking in each word and thinking about what they mean to the person speaking. You're not thinking about what you'll say in response or waiting to jump in with a situation you've been in that was similar. You're *only* listening.

Focused listening often requires a pause between when the person stops talking and when you respond. We're not used to any kind of pause, but it's really okay to sit in the quiet between thoughts for a few seconds. That pause conveys to the person that you were focused on listening.

Statements like, "Tell me more about that" or "Wow. What did that look like?" can help the person continue their own exploration of the situation.

Focused listening provides space for people to work through issues on their own. This requires you to let go of solving the problem for them, or even intervening in their process of talking it through. Encouraging them to work it through is the best support you can offer—in this moment and for the future when they need to solve problems on their own.

This isn't easy. I'm a big problem-solver. People in leadership positions are, by nature, problem-solvers. I always have lots of my own experiences that I just *know* would be helpful to people. But I've learned (sometimes the hard way) that sharing my experiences can be counter-productive. Most of the time, the best thing I can do is concentrate on my focused listening and let the other person talk. (This is especially true if you are the parent of a teenager.)

When we were teaching focused listening in one of our classes, a participant described his favorite boss like this: "I'd go into his office to tell him about something I was grappling with, knowing that he was very wise and experienced and that he'd give me the answer. It wasn't until years later that I realized how little he actually said when I was in his office. I'd talk and he'd nod and say, "Tell me more about that." And I would tell him more and, eventually, a light bulb would come on in my head and I would say, 'Oh! I know! This is what I need to do.' And I would leave his office feeling like he was the wisest man in the world. I asked it him about it after I'd been gone from the company for a few years and he said, 'If you let people talk and if you really listen as they're talking, nine times out of ten they'll come to their own answers, and those answers are always better than the ones I would have given them.'"

Level 3—Epic Listening. The third type of listening is epic listening. This is the deepest level of listening and it is the level that most requires an expanded capacity for being instead of doing.

Epic listening is the level of listening where you begin to really tune in to the emotional state of the person talking. You hear their words, but you also get beyond the words to understand what's beneath the words, what might be motivating that person to speak those words. Epic listening is most often useful in times of intense effort, crisis, sadness, agitation, joy, or pride.

Epic listening enables us to get at the *real* issue, not spend our time dealing with the *symptoms* of the issue. Epic listening can save tremendous time and effort.

One of the participants in our training described her successful experience with epic listening and how it saved her time. One of her direct reports came into her office agitated and ready for a fight. He told her that his counterpart in the other division wasn't getting her work done, and that was making it impossible for him to get his work done. He was angry about the timing of the workflow and how it was impossible to get things done in the time allotted, how his people were frustrated, and how the overall goal was ridiculous anyway. (Have you ever been on the receiving end of that kind of rant? I certainly have, more than once.)

This leader recognized an opportunity for epic listening and consciously practiced tuning in to his words while also tuning in to the emotions and motivations behind his words. She listened quietly while he told her about all the things everyone was doing wrong and about what was ridiculous about everything in the company. When he finished, rather than jump to solving (or telling him to stop whining, which is often my first inclination), she calmly replied, "It sounds to me like you're really overwhelmed."

He sighed, sank into his chair, and said, "I am really overwhelmed."

They were then able to have a conversation about how to tackle his sense of overwhelm, some of which included how to deal with his counterpart and his people's frustrations. The conversation was designed to alleviate his sense of overwhelm so that he would be able to deal with the situations swirling around him.

Each level of listening—faux, focused, or epic—is a conscious choice. Now that you know that there are three different levels of listening, and that each has its place, you can choose which to use when.

Start simply, by noticing how often, when someone else is talking, you're thinking about what you'll say in response. You might be surprised.

* * *

The choice to *Embark* on the path toward being the kind of leader you want to be means taking responsibility for your choices about how you show up.

It means acknowledging the complexity that surrounds you and embracing the uncertainty that comes with complexity.

On a practical level, it means talking less and listening more.

CHAPTER 2

EXPLORE

In the shift from doing to being, it's critical that we *Explore* our own personal story. I'm not asking you to unpack your relationship with your mother or plumb the depths of that game-losing shot when you were a senior in high school. This is not therapy. What I'm asking you to do is to take a look at the experiences, circumstances, people and opportunities that shaped you because they continue to shape you—for good and for not-so-good.

I like to call this "owning your own shit," because let's face it—we all have stuff that we carry with us. It has incredible power over how we show up—*especially* if we're not aware of it.

PERFECTLY OURSELVES AT ALL TIMES

A few years ago I was sitting at a long table with my friends from college, celebrating twenty-five years since we'd graduated. I was smiling as I observed each of us interacting in the *exact same ways* we did when we were in college together. My friend John turned to me and said, "It's a good thing we're all so perfectly ourselves at all times."

That's it!

In the end, we are all *perfectly ourselves at all times*. In many ways, it's impossible for us *not* to be ourselves. What I've learned, in my own experience and from many many conversations with leaders who are exploring their own personal story, is that it's very expedient and often helpful to be perfectly ourselves, and then sometimes it's decidedly not helpful and, in the long run, not expedient.

I am the oldest child in my family and the only girl. I have two younger brothers. My dad travelled most weeks when I was growing up, relegating me to the role of "other grown up" in the house. I am *very* responsible ... all the time. I do annoying things like automatically take things that people are carrying and carry them myself.

I'm a big believer in not asking anyone to do anything I wouldn't do myself. (That one comes up when I ask myself who I want to be and my answer is my dad.)

The problem is I do *everything*—often well beyond what I should ask anyone else to do. Because of this, one of the key challenges of working with me is that I do everything—not because I actively think others can't do it—but because it's my default mode, my natural state.

This hyper sense of responsibility can be a great thing. I'm responsible, reliable and *man*, I get shit done. The problem is that it actively keeps other people from taking responsibility. My team is left with the dregs of work that I can't see or that I haven't automatically added to my to do list.

This can lead me to over-commit—individually and on behalf of my company. Sometimes I have to call on my team to take things on in a major time crunch because I couldn't get something done. If I'd moved out of my default mode and gotten others involved from the beginning, they would be learning and growing, I wouldn't be overwhelmed and we would all work at a smarter pace. And I'm sure we'd do even better work.

I worked with one CEO whose child had been very ill as an infant. In response, she developed a sense of hyper-vigilance that she eventually began applying to all aspects of her life. She was constantly scanning for danger to the point of paralysis. What began as a helpful and necessary response to an ill child ended up being a terrible burden on everyone who worked with her. It wasn't until she realized that she was applying the same hyper-vigilance required to keep her child safe to everyday decisions and interactions that she was able to adjust her behavior and return to a more balanced approach.

Another CEO with whom I've worked was very proud of his role as peacemaker in his family. He had always been the person in the family who could bring people together and get everyone on the same page. Those skills had helped to propel him to his role as CEO. As he explored his personal story, he realized that he sometimes waited to act on a decision until he could get everyone aligned around the decision and that that was creating delays and causing problems for his company.

The shift from doing to being means recognizing that we are all, inevitably, "perfectly ourselves at all times." Sometimes that's great ... and sometimes it's not.

TRUE TO OURSELVES BUT NOT NECESSARILY *PERFECTLY* OURSELVES

William Shakespeare wrote these words more than four hundred years ago:

> *"This above all: to thine own self be true,*
> *And it must follow, as the night the day,*
> *Thou canst not then be false to any man."*
> –William Shakespeare, *Hamlet*

"To thine own self be true" *is* actually the powerful place from which great leadership comes.

You know those moments ... the times when you feel in your gut that you've just absolutely *got* this. (Notice the smile on your face right now as you contemplate it.)

I know that when I'm being true to myself, I make decisions more quickly. I have tough conversations more readily and successfully. I become clear about what needs to get done and I am able to communicate it to others. I have a sense of clarity that is not only powerful for me; it creates a field of magnetism that draws people in.

How often do you operate from that place of clarity? How consistently are you able to tap into that powerful center where you just *know* what to do or say, almost without thinking?

Being true to ourselves means knowing who we are—the good, the bad and the ugly. If we don't know who we are then we can't really make a conscious choice to be true to ourselves, can we?

Our personal stories are a *gold mine* of opportunities to get clear about who we are and what we care about. Our core values and the deeply rooted places from which we authentically show up are embedded in our personal stories—past and present.

Once we've identified those core values and the places from which we authentically show up, we can make the choice to be true to ourselves while simultaneously acknowledging and actively working against the parts of ourselves that are deeply held but not necessarily useful in a particular role or situation—those default modes that trip us up. We're able to choose the best of ourselves.

This is the *foundation* of the power in the shift from doing to being.

INVITING OTHERS TO HOLD US ACCOUNTABLE

One of the greatest challenges of staying out of our default modes is that they're *unconscious*. We have a hard time seeing when we're falling into them. They are simply our natural state; they're just how we operate. (And again, they've often worked well for us.)

If you want to accelerate your path to great leadership, you'll need to find ways to hold yourself accountable. Identifying our own unhelpful default modes is a first step, but if we truly want to move more quickly toward great leadership, we've got to share these default modes with others and ask them to step in to hold us accountable.

To offset my default mode of hyper-responsibility, I share this challenge overtly with my team. Sometimes I tell people how it ties to my personal story and sometimes I just claim it as one of my default modes that can get me (and therefore my company) into trouble.

When I share this story or describe this default mode, I make a request. I ask the people around me to push me when they want more responsibility and/or when they see me taking on too much without thinking about the impact it's having on me and the company.

While I was writing this very section of this book I got an email from a member of my team:

"Our processes for hiring and onboarding aren't very well developed yet and we realize that you may be concerned about bringing on new people because of that. I propose that you let us begin drafting some of the processes... maybe even some possible interview questions since we're going to need to interview people soon."

Our company has an impending need and my team knows, because I've been transparent about this particular unhelpful default mode of mine, that I have added this task to my (very long) "to do" list. And because they're aware of that tendency on my part, there's an opening - an invitation - for them to jump in and take responsibility. I wrote back and said, "Go for it. Thank you." And I know they'll do a great job of getting that started.

We all have these default modes. They are part of our personality and inherent in our temperament. These natural ways of operating are influenced by our gender and race and where and how we grew up. They're amplified or diminished by our current circumstances. They are often our greatest strengths and, in their shadow side, our greatest weaknesses. Naming these default modes and inviting others to hold us accountable when we're slipping into them is a powerful way to be true to ourselves but not always *perfectly* ourselves.

THE CEO SECRET FOR *EXPLORE*

Exploring our personal story enables us to understand how our experiences affect our decisions, actions and interactions.

I call this "owning your own shit."

TOOL 1:
KNOW YOUR STORY

Knowing our personal story gives us insight into the values that are at the foundation of our actions and it gives us access to the default modes that might be holding us back.

Our personal stories are shaped by many many factors—where we grew up, how many siblings we had, our ethnic or religious background and culture, our race and gender, things we may not even consider. I happen to be six feet tall. Being a six-foot-tall woman has shaped my experience in the world in significant ways.

There are also moments—conversations and interactions we've had, things we've loved and things we've hated, turning points that changed our path, opportunities taken and lost, ideas that set us on fire—that made us who we are. Those continue to influence how we think, act, and interact.

Exploring our personal story is a way of bringing our unconscious reactions to the surface and building a strong connection to our best self. By exploring how we got to where we are, we can more readily own where we want to go. We can decide what's useful and what's not.

So, how can you think about your personal story in a way that accelerates your path toward great leadership? Begin by completing the following statements:

One turning point or peak moment for me in my *personal* **life was...** (*Think of a specific event or time of challenge,* *insight or opportunity; or a specific idea or insight—describe it in some detail.)*

That was important because… *(Think about what you learned from it and/or how it changed you or your future from that point.)*

One turning point or peak moment for me in my *professional* **life was…** *(Think of a specific event or time of challenge, insight, or opportunity; or a specific idea or insight—describe it in some detail.)*

That was important because… *(Think about what you learned from it and/or how it changed you or your future from that point.)*

The people or ideas that helped me navigate my turning points were… *(Be specific. Describe the people and how you knew them, or the ideas and how you discovered them, and think about how they helped you.)*

I would describe the family I grew up in as… *(What's your family dynamic? Are you close? All very different? Similar? Caring, outgoing, argumentative, loud…?)*

You would recognize this about my family if you saw us… *(Give an example that demonstrates your description of your family.)*

My role in my family was/is… *(Give a specific example of how you filled this role—think of a particular situation or event that demonstrates it.)*

The most fun I had growing up was… *(Think of family events or games you played with siblings or friends, trips you took, favorite toys or pastimes.)*

I would say that growing up in my family taught me...
(Think about the family's values; insights about yourself; the roles of education, work, faith, family; how success was measured, etc.)

What makes me happy now is...

I think my personal story paints a picture of me as...

Take a few minutes to really contemplate these statements. Try answering them on the computer or jot notes in a notebook. If you want to download the full set of questions, you can find them on our website: FindingTimeToLead.com.

There's something satisfying about exploring your story, and there's something powerful about owning it—all of it.

So, what do you see? Who are the people who influenced you—for good or not-so-good? (Sometimes we learn the most from the people we don't want to be like.) What are the moments, interactions, and choices that helped to shape who you are?

A lot of the people who have done this exercise end up sending notes to parents or coaches or friends—people who positively influenced who they are today. If you came up with a few of those, why not write them a note of thanks? You'll be glad you did.

- What influence might those people and experiences be having on you now?
- What are you bringing with you to the role of CEO?
- Which of these things are positive and which might be detrimental?

- Which are strengths until they are over-used to the point of becoming impediments to your success?
- What habitual responses do you default to without even thinking? (Like when I go to the store with my daughter and she picks something up that she wants and I automatically—and completely unconsciously—take it from her to carry it for her, until my arms are completely full and she's not carrying anything.)

Once you've answered these statements, look back over them. If you're willing, share them with someone who listens well.

As you consider your story, list some of the values that are inherent in your story. Some examples might be: hard work, intellectual curiosity, family, giving back, or independence. (You can find a more comprehensive list of values at FindingTimeToLead.com.)

Think about the people you identified as having a positive influence. When you ask yourself, *Who do I want to be right now?* are you like them? Identifying your core values and considering the people you want to be like gives you a platform for choosing your best self in every situation.

And the really good news? Showing up as your best self requires only a split second longer than *not* showing up as your best self.

TOOL 2:
AVOID BEING *PERFECTLY* YOURSELF

Identifying our default modes enables us to distinguish between when they are helpful and when they are not. Our unconscious brain *loves* these default modes. You know, those regular ways of being and reacting that are so familiar that we can just drop into them without thinking. They're quick and easy and, often, they're exactly what we need... until they're not.

The trick is to be *aware* of our default modes—which are often influenced by our personal story—so that, when they're *not* what we need, we're able to make a different choice.

A CEO with whom I've worked described his ability to almost immediately and "pretty accurately" pinpoint a person's weaknesses. That default mode could be a very real advantage when he was considering how to get the best out of people, but it could also keep him from seeing possibilities in people. He recognized that he needed to expand his view so that he could both utilize this strength and, at the same time, temper it to keep from pigeonholing people to the point that he missed opportunities.

What are your default modes?

Was competition important in your family or where you grew up? You may have a fierce sense of competition and a desire to win that has given you the drive that got you here. Is it still serving you? Under what circumstances might that competitiveness not serve you now?

Were you always the smartest? Were you at the top of your class? A straight-A student? How do you respond when you don't have immediate, measurable feedback about something?

What might you be looking for to replace it? Can you get comfortable with not having immediate, quantifiable feedback?

Those are only some of the default modes that we humans pick up in an effort to interact with the world around us in productive ways. Often, they're our greatest strengths… and sometimes they're also our greatest weaknesses.

Take a minute or two to reflect on your personal story and write down a few default modes that seem pertinent to how you show up. Check them with people close to you—they'll know.

TOOL 3:
INVITE ACCOUNTABILITY

Let's say you've identified one or two default modes that you recognize may not serve you, especially in your role as CEO. How will you hold yourself accountable for not slipping right back into them? After all, these are *default* modes. They're ways we behave without thinking, and that makes it very difficult—nearly impossible at times—for us to catch ourselves and do something different.

Sharing our default modes with colleagues and requesting that they point out when they see us operating in those default mode creates accountability around a response or behavior that is unconscious for us. It also invites others to step in and offset our default modes with their own strengths.

My team knows to step up and take on work, even when I haven't given it to them, because they know that I don't naturally hand things off. That dynamic has been important for us.

Your accountability partners could be fellow members of your executive team, a coach or mentor, a group of other CEOs, or a spouse or friend. The key thing is to articulate your default mode to someone else and ask them specifically to help you watch out for it.

Saying out loud that you've identified something you do that, when left unchecked, might be detrimental to your company may sound crazy. Why would you admit that? Why would you say that out loud to people?

Because you *own* it. Because you know that, in the best interest of your company and on the path to the leader you want to be, you will have to admit that you're not perfect.

Acknowledging, from a place of self-awareness and ownership, that you're working on something is *powerful*. Not only do you demonstrate the kind of self-awareness that great leaders display, you're modeling it for others.

Wouldn't it be refreshing if your vice president for sales said to you, "I'm really competitive and I always want to win—pretty much at any cost. Because of that, I sometimes make promises that I know we can't keep—just so I can win the business. I recognize that that's creating all kinds of problems for our engineers. I need to be more thoughtful and not get so caught up in winning. I wanted to let you know this so that, when I'm in the throes of pitching a deal, you know you may need to talk me down so that I don't over-promise."

Are you thinking that scenario is impossible?

If you haven't led by doing this type of thing yourself, then you're right... it is probably impossible for those around you to do it.

* * *

Our personal story influences how we act and interact—in every moment. In choosing to *Explore* our personal story, we can "own our own shit." Inviting accountability from colleagues, a coach, a friend or a partner enables us to move beyond our default modes so that we can be true to ourselves without always being *perfectly* ourselves.

PART TWO

THE SECOND SHIFT
FROM KNOWING TO UNDERSTANDING

Shifting from knowing to understanding opens our minds and expands our capacity for engagement, making every question, conversation, disagreement, and action an opportunity for learning.

There are two practices that will support you in the shift from knowing to understanding—*Expand* and *Engage*, which we'll explore in the next two chapters.

CHAPTER 3

EXPAND

Sadly, our brains sometimes work against us when we're trying to make the shift from knowing to understanding. That is why this shift begins with knowing how our brains work and leveraging that knowledge to *Expand* our capacity for courageous action in the face of discomfort.

As humans, our brains are hard-wired for the status quo. We *crave* predictability. It makes us feel safe. When predictability is replaced with possibility we get uncomfortable. When predictability is replaced with outright uncertainty, we get hostile. Even if you're one of those people who "thrives on change," there is a point at which change, the glimpse of the new, awakens your lizard brain and you are forced into your own doubts, fears, and a chorus of second guesses.

And yet... it is at the edges of our experience, in times of change or disruption, that real learning and progress occurs.

Making the shift from knowing to understanding requires us to *Expand* our thinking. When we're seeking to understand and not just to know, our questions are bigger, our perspectives are more encompassing. In this space, we develop the ability to hold the tension of opposites and ask, "What if?"

OUR LIZARD BRAIN

Our brains don't like it when things are unknown and unpredictable. The part of our brain that has kept us alive as a species rules our response to unpredictability and the danger it might create. When I say this part of our brain rules, I mean it creates *unconscious* rules.

Remember our brilliant CEO who responded with "Hell no!" when his business partner offered an initial settlement in the early stages of their negotiation? That was his lizard brain responding. The small (yet very powerful) part of the brain that controls our immediate fight or flight reactions is what said, "Hell no!" That was *not* the part of the brain that is able to *Expand* to take in new information and rationally respond to it.

Our lizard brain reactions don't have to be that dramatic. But those defensive reactions we sometimes have in the face of criticism or when things aren't going well? Lizard brain.

Toddlers are the best example of the lizard brain. Toddlers are like the lizard brain laid bare. A friend of mine was having a back and forth with her three-year-old son about bedtime. He wasn't ready for bed, but it was definitely time for bed. When she told him that it was time for bed, he—like any good toddler—said, "No." She said, "It is time for bed now." And he said, "No," more loudly. She responded, "If you don't go upstairs now, you can't have a cupcake tomorrow." At which point, he got really mad. He clenched his little fists, screwed up his face, sputtered a couple of times, and then yelled as loudly as he could, "To infinity *and beyond*!" which is, of course, what Buzz Lightyear says in *Toy Story*.

I feel that way sometimes. I'm frustrated or angry and I can't think of the right thing to say. I just want to shout something that feels satisfying. We are grown-ups, though, so we don't get to do that. Our "To infinity *and beyond*!" moments are much more subtle—and potentially much more harmful.

I've worked with a number of CEOs who are very proud of their "open door policy." They actively encourage people to come to them with feedback and thoughts about their experiences in the company—both the good and bad. That is all great, until someone takes the CEO up on their invitation and the CEO responds defensively.

If the CEO responds to feedback offered with phrases like "What the heck do you mean!?" or "This is the first *I've* heard of it" or "Well, that may be how it looks from *your* perspective, but not from *my* perspective" or, another good one, "Are you sure that's not just because..." ("... you haven't been here very long," "... you're a woman," "... he's just having a bad day..."—fill in the blank).

Those kinds of defensive (or outright hostile) reactions come from your lizard brain. Most of the time, when you regret having said something, that means that it came from your lizard brain, not from the part of your brain that is able to *Expand* to take in all kinds of information.

HERE'S HOW IT WORKS

Our brain evolved over millions of years. It began with the brain stem—also called the lizard brain (which functions the same way in humans as it does in a gecko). The brain stem controls breathing, heart rate, sleeping and waking.

Sitting on top of the brain stem is the "mammalian brain," which is all about survival. In his book, *Brain Rules,* John Medina says that "most of the functions of the mammalian brain involve what some researchers call the 'four Fs': fighting, feeding, fleeing and... reproductive behavior."

The amygdala allows us to feel rage, fear, or pleasure. The amygdala is also the part of the brain that connects current experiences with past experiences of rage, fear, or pleasure.

There are layers of the brain that are responsible for memory and sensory signals.

And then there is the cortex. This is the most recent and uniquely human part of our brain. It is the seat of rational thought; the part of our brain that generates the brilliant connections, snappy retorts, poetic language, and profound thoughts that make us human. It is the part of the human brain that has enabled us to learn and adapt, and to create solutions to problems in such a way that we now find ourselves at the top of the food chain.

Why is this important to know?

The ability to think clearly is critical to being able to

Expand our perspective and choose our response, but our initial responses come from those parts of our brain that developed early. They flood our system with the chemicals that put us in "fight or flight" mode. When that happens, our access to the thinking part of our brain is *literally* cut off.

This explains why, ten minutes after an argument or altercation, we can think of the exact right thing to say. The thinking part of our brain that is able to come up with that snappy retort was *literally* not accessible to us in the heat of the moment when our brain was flooded.

So, how do we accelerate access to the thinking part of our brain? Easy. Take a deep breath. There's a reason we teach preschoolers to take a breath and count to ten before they *do* anything when they're upset about something. It's pure biology.

We'll talk more about how taking a deep breath helps in the tools section of this chapter. Meanwhile, let's pretend you've breathed deeply and you've got your wits about you again. You've still got challenges.

CREATING SPACE FOR "WHAT IF?"

When we're coming from the perspective of a need to *know*, we're more likely to operate from our lizard brain and we can easily get trapped. Our need to know can lock us into seeing things as a choice between two ideas or perspectives: "I'm either in charge or I'm not" and "That person either gets it or they don't."

Have you ever found yourself in one of those no-win situations? You know, the ones where you know there's no decision that's going to work for everyone and you feel like everyone is looking to you to decide, to choose one path or the other.

We long for the simplicity of *one right answer*, a choice so clear it's a case of black and white, so obvious to us and to everyone else what the "right" answer is. But the reality is that we live in the gray area. We lead in the space between black and white, where there are multiple "right" answers. We operate in a world where things look different, depending on where we stand, in a world where predictability is rare.

Because of that, in order to hold the tension of opposites—we have to *Expand* our thinking, to recognize that *this* and *that* can be true simultaneously. This perspective is necessary if we're going to get to a *best* answer instead of getting to a temporary "right" answer.

Our drive for short-term solutions instead of long-term resolutions creates all kinds of headaches that we have to clean up later—which usually takes *way* more time than if we had pushed through to the long-term resolution in the first place.

This isn't easy. Holding the tension of opposites requires courage and the ability to be in uncertainty. We like the certainty of right or wrong, left or right, this or that, yes or no, but that need for certainty, for one right answer, limits our capacity to be creative. It constructs a binary system that gives us only two options, or an unsatisfying compromise between the two.

In companies, this plays out in the "sales and marketing vs. engineering" scenario, in the "finance vs. service delivery" dialogue, and in "short-term efficiency vs. long-term efficacy" decisions.

When we're able to hold this tension, to recognize that two points of view can be simultaneously real, important, and true, it creates space for the possibility of a third way, a creative possibility that meets the needs of both. Holding this tension creates the opportunity for real dialogue and creative problem-solving. It creates an opening for "what if."

LIFE AT THE EDGES

As CEO, you are constantly at the edge. It's your job to lead your company to the next level, to grow it, to innovate, to move into new markets or create new products, to build or rebuild a great culture. We don't move through and past those edges without discomfort.

My team and I were working in close partnership with a CEO who had a vision for his company as the kind of place where people took responsibility for themselves and their work and where everyone deeply engaged with others from a place of real passion and care—for the individual people and for the organization. To support that vision, we introduced a series of leadership programs.

We focused on leadership as a personal practice and we enrolled a small group in one of the programs—the CEO and twelve other people, some of whom were managers and some of whom were not.

Over the course of a year, we trained the program participants to be more accountable, to be braver about speaking up, and to be able to speak up in productive ways. The CEO saw tremendous growth in his own leadership capacity and in the capacity of others in the program. He began to see his fellow participants stepping up and taking responsibility for themselves and the company in new ways. It was working.

And then, toward the end of that year of training, one of the Senior Leadership Team members burst into the CEO's office and exclaimed, "I've had about enough of this leadership bullshit!"

Ah-ha! It really *was* working. We could tell because the system was beginning to adjust to new ideas and ways of interacting. Not surprisingly (because we humans like things to be predictable), that adjustment was causing tension and some very real pushback.

At that moment, the CEO had a choice to make. He could have called me and said, "Nope, this is upsetting my top people. We can't handle this kind of disruption. We can't do any more of this."

Instead, we sat down over coffee and talked about how we could support his people through the change. He was able to *Expand* his thinking to see that it was not a simple choice between whether to continue the training and risk upsetting his senior leadership team or to stop the training.

It was true that the changes were going to create challenges, and it was also true that it was producing the results he had hoped for. What if we continued the training in spite of the tension it created? What if we more actively supported the senior leadership team through the transition?

It wouldn't be easy—for them or for the CEO. He was taking some serious heat as people adjusted to new ways of being together, as they expanded their whole notion of leadership. It wasn't clear yet what the new system would look like. He didn't *know* what the outcome would be, but he *understood* that it was a change in the right direction.

The CEO had the personal courage to stay the course—even in the face of discomfort and outright opposition. He recognized that there was a space between when we commit to something and when the outcomes start becoming visible. It is in that *space between* that leaders really have to show up—not because they know the outcome, but because they are able to hold the tension between where they are now and where they want to be.

Leaders act with courage in the face of the disequilibrium that naturally comes with any kind of change. They hold the space for possibility while those around them may be struggling to let go of predictability. They work to *understand*, recognizing that they cannot really *know*. And they tame their lizard brain to make space for the new.

Let's explore some tools you can use to *Expand* your thinking as you make the shift from knowing to understanding.

THE CEO SECRET FOR *EXPAND*

Being a CEO means living at the edge—pushing yourself and your company to the next level. Edges, because they are the places where learning happens, inevitably create disequilibrium and discomfort.

When we *Expand* our thinking, we're able to move past our lizard brain, hold the tension of opposites, and ask, "What if...?"—especially in times of disequilibrium and discomfort.

TOOL 1:
TAKE A BREATH AND COUNT TO TEN

The reason we teach preschoolers to take a breath and count to ten is because it helps us connect more quickly with the thinking part of our brain after it has been flooded by the chemicals that trigger our fight-or-flight response.

Our lizard brain has a *million* stories to tell us about how terrible we are or how awful it will be when we fail. (It is, after all, our lizard brain's job to keep us from doing things that could be dangerous in any way.) If you want to respond to people well, if you want to make bold decisions and be open to opportunity, then you need to get to the thinking part of your brain—quickly. How do you get there? Simple: Before you do anything else, take a deep breath and count to ten.

The CEO who responded, "Hell no! We're not doing that" at a delicate moment during negotiations? That was his lizard brain talking; that was his fight or flight response to an immediate threat to the company he was building and to how he had imagined his future. If he had taken a deep breath, he might have been able to access the thinking part of his brain and thus been able to respond with a request for some time to consider the offer. That one deep breath might have changed the trajectory of his company.

You can't *Expand* your thinking and make the shift from knowing to understanding if you can't access the part of your brain that is able to think rationally, *especially* when you're in the midst of a challenge. And you can't expect people to follow you into the unknown if you're not leading with the kind of courage and conviction that is made possible only by being able to access your whole brain.

TOOL 2:
EMBRACE DISEQUILIBRIUM

Moving into something new creates *disequilibrium*. Our past ways of understanding things are no longer directly relevant. We have to create entirely new frameworks for understanding the situation in which we now find ourselves. We have to move past our lizard brain and *Expand* our thinking.

Let's say, as a native English speaker, that you're trying to learn Spanish. You have to learn new words for the words you already know, but you can apply the same letters and similar sounds from knowing English. By contrast, if you're trying to learn Chinese, every character and sound are *new*. What you already know isn't applicable to this new learning. It requires something completely new and different.

Our brains find this very confusing and challenging. It puts us in a state of disequilibrium, where the learning is huge and exhilarating and scary all at the same time. A colleague of mine likens it to the huge rush you feel when you head down that first big hill on a roller coaster.

But learning happens when we're in disequilibrium, when we're headed down that roller coaster hill. Learning and change are about letting go of the status quo and taking the next step. If we're not able to embrace that feeling of fear, exhilaration, excitement, and possibility, then we're not going to be able to lead our company into the next phase.

Unlike the roller coaster hill, though, we don't move through disequilibrium in a blink; it takes time.

Chaos theory offers what I think is the most comforting framework for this idea that there is discomfort before we get to the next place. In chaos theory, systems have to break down before they can reorder, before the new can emerge. For example, when a tree falls, it takes time to for that tree to decay. It takes a long time for it to become the soil from which a new tree can grow.

I call this time of disequilibrium and discomfort the narrow part of the tunnel. A CEO with whom I work uses the image of an hour glass. Picture the sand moving from the top to the bottom of the hourglass through the narrow middle where it's slow going—everything jams up and the flow isn't smooth. That is a time of deep discomfort and fear. It is a moment when understanding is far more important than knowing... precisely *because* the outcome can't be known.

It's also the moment when we want to put the genie back in the bottle, turn the hourglass back over, and avoid the discomfort of allowing things to break down without knowing exactly how they will reorder.

Consider your personal story. What experiences come to mind when you think about your own personal and professional peak moments and turning points? Were the outcomes clear from the beginning? Was there a point at which you felt like turning back? How do *you* ride that roller coaster of disequilibrium? What does it look like for you to support people through their own disequilibrium?

You, as the CEO, are holding space for people to be in discomfort, in the thrashing mess of the unknown. Your job is not to minimize the discomfort or to make it go away. Your job is to model how to be in the disequilibrium and discomfort that learning and growing produce, to show up in such a way that people can have an example to help them handle their own discomfort, push their own edges, and evolve—individually and together.

TOOL 3:
HOLD THE TENSION OF OPPOSITES
AND ASK "WHAT IF...?"

Holding the tension of opposites—acknowledging that two things can be true at the same time—creates space for us to ask "what if" questions.

As a leader, you are in a position to take in seemingly opposing points of view and introduce the highest aspirations of the whole. Your vision for the company, for how people will work together, for the kind of service you strive to provide for customers is a powerful tool.

Let's consider the ever-present marketing/sales vs. engineering/product development dilemma. There appears to be a choice to be made between placing the emphasis on one or the other. We do our best to balance the two. We picture them on a straight line and try to find the right point between the two. Marketing/sales and engineering/product development may be equally important to our business and to the customer, but the exact mid-point between the two probably isn't the right balance.

Think about your wildest dreams for your company. Consider what kind of service you hope to provide for customers; think about how, in a perfect world, your people would work together to make that happen.

Picture a triangle, with marketing and engineering across from each other on the bottom points of the triangle and picture your highest aspirations as the top point on the triangle. In this image, you and your team have lots of space in between the three points to develop creative solutions. Your choices are not only one point on a line.

You can introduce new possibilities into the conversation by asking "what if" questions, like this: *What if* we were able to meet the needs of marketing/sales *and* engineering/product development *and* build the kinds of relationships with customers that inspire them to talk to everyone in our industry about how great we are?" That's a much more interesting and exciting conversation than, "How can we meet the needs of both marketing/sales and engineering/product development?"

If you want to build a company where everyone is working for the good of the larger whole, where everyone is encouraged to make a meaningful contribution to the company's success, where customers become inspired advocates for your brand, then painting a picture of those aspirations and bringing them into the conversation can effectively call out the best in each of the players involved. Offering "what ifs" that tie the issue to your highest aspirations for the company instantly makes space for possibilities. It challenges everyone involved to think differently.

Challenge yourself to articulate your own highest aspirations for your company—not only the growth rate or sales volume (although those are important). Make a list of what you want your people, your customers, and your community to say about your company and its work. This will give you easy access to the "what if" questions that create new options and opportunities. (If you'd like more questions to help guide you through this, you can find them at FindingTimeToLead.com.)

* * *

When we're in the mindset of understanding instead of knowing, we're able to stay calm through the disequilibrium that happens at the edges.

We can tame our lizard brain in order to access the thinking part of our brain that enables us to *Expand* our thinking, hold the tension of opposites, and introduce the possibilities created by asking, "What if...?"

CHAPTER 4

ENGAGE

We know that disengaged employees are a disaster for productivity, service, innovation, and loyalty. A 2015 Gallup poll of more than 80,000 working adults found that 50.8% of them were "not engaged" and 17.2% were "actively disengaged." That's 68% of working adults who feel disengaged at work, leaving a dismal 32% who do feel engaged.

Imagine how much lost potential, productivity, innovation, and fulfillment is lost because of that 68%. You don't want that to be true of your company. There's too much opportunity to even *consider* wasting that much potential. And, besides, aren't you the kind of leader who *wants* the people in your company to be engaged? To feel fulfilled in their work? To bring their best selves to what they do every day? That's good for business *and* it's good for people, families, and communities.

"Our basic human need to be understood, respected and missed when we're gone doesn't get satisfied easily. As a result, when genuine connection is offered, it's often taken."
~ Seth Godin, *The Icarus Deception*

So how do we lead in such a way that we can truly *Engage* our people?

There are hundreds of books and articles about employee engagement. They are full of tips and tools and things you can say and do. It usually boils down to communication. If you can communicate well, people will be engaged. This implies that saying the right thing will lead to engagement and commitment.

That is partially true. What you say matters *a lot*. How you say it is also important. The words you use are critical. But that's still not enough...

THE PARKING LOT MAFIA

In the absence of information, people make shit up.

You know it's true. You've seen it happen. Sometimes—even when there's *a lot* of information—people *still* make shit up.

It's not that they're necessarily *trying* to make stuff up (although sometimes they are); it's that their brains are searching for explanations for whatever is happening. That's how our brains work. We *need* explanations. We want to understand things for ourselves.

I've worked with a lot of schools. In schools, the parking lot is the equivalent of the water cooler. There are always some people who tend to hang out in the parking lot and complain about everything. We call them "the parking lot mafia."

The water cooler, the coffee pot, the parking lot, instant messaging—it doesn't matter the locale—the fact is, human beings actively seek out those who can explain things, who can validate our perspective, who can jump with us into our point of view. We look for genuine connection—even if it's negative.

You may think that conversations among parents in the school parking lot are mild compared to what we experience in a corporate setting, but I would invite you to picture your most vocal and destructive employee or customer. Now imagine how he or she would interact with you if you were responsible for educating his child, and then imagine that his child has a disability. These are not mild conversations.

I encountered one particularly destructive parking lot mafia that had decided that the principal of the school was inaccessible and unfriendly, so they made themselves very busy telling everyone that the principal was inaccessible and unfriendly. They created a narrative—and it went viral.

Narratives are the stories we tell ourselves and each other. They are how we express the things we think we've come to know. If there is no counter-narrative—nothing to offset the prevailing narrative—then one particular narrative usually becomes dominant, and it can lift us up or tear us down.

In truth, the principal of that school was very friendly, but also fairly shy. She had met with several families and spoken with other families in impromptu moments when they had stopped by her office. She loved her one-on-one time with families, but large groups weren't her natural environment, so she avoided the crush of drop-off and pick-up times and parent gatherings. Because she wasn't visible to parents, their narrative about her being unfriendly and inaccessible took hold. Every time she wasn't at an event or saying hello at drop-off in the morning, the parking lot mafia group had the opportunity to talk about how she wasn't there, which reinforced their message that she was unfriendly and inaccessible. Those parents were *very* engaged in the life of the school, but it wasn't positive engagement.

Can you bring to mind the people in your company who have taken on a similar role? Every group or organization has them and, very often, we give them the power to create the narratives that become who we are as an organization— by not stepping in and presenting a different, more positive narrative. We'll explore this more in the third tool for *Engage*: Support the Counter-Narrative.

LEADING FOR ENGAGEMENT

Leading for engagement looks different than our traditional idea of leadership in which we believe that the leaders have the information and knowledge we need to do our work. In this vision of leadership, leaders believe that if they convey the information well enough, people will be committed and ready to get to work.

It turns out, though, that leadership is a *team* sport. Leading is a social process. The coach builds a championship culture, inspires her players to work hard, teaches them plays and positions, and then, when the players are on the field, they have to respond in their own ways to the exact, unpredictable thing that is happening in that moment.

The coach can't possibly be in everyone's ear telling them what to do when they're on the field playing the game. She has to build in the players a commitment to working hard and an intense desire to win. As the coach, she has to provide the information and training that her players need in order to make good decisions and work together when they're in the moment, on the field. She creates and reinforces the narrative about who they are as a team.

Once the game starts, it's up to the players to notice and respond on their own to what's happening on the field, to signal each other when one person has a move or a shot or an idea, and to respond in that moment. They're able to see what makes sense, given the immediate circumstances, and react, both individually and as a team. No one has to tell them what to do in those moments. They are in motion, not waiting for instructions. Each team member is doing what they need to do in order for the team to succeed. The quarterback who makes that pass couldn't have made it unless every other player was doing what they needed to be doing, and doing it well.

Have you ever watched a jazz band perform? It's remarkable how much communication happens between and among the players at the same time that they're perform-ing. They're all individually leading, taking turns leading, and leading together to produce something remarkable.

The same thing happens at your company.

People are in constant motion. They're not waiting for instruc-tion. The frameworks and culture we create enable them to act and interact in the best interest of the whole... or not.

Leading for engagement is about making sense of our work together, so that everyone can operate at their highest point of contribution. Information becomes a free-flowing resource from which we can all draw meaning. There is no perfect message from the leader that will instantaneously move us to engagement and commitment. We get there together.

PINEAPPLE TABLES

Did you ever play the telephone game? One person whis-pers something to a second person and the second person whispers the message to a third person, all around a circle, until the whispered message gets back to the person who started it. We play this in my family and *never* have I wit-nessed the same message coming back to the person who started it. My favorite was when the first person started with the phrase "blueberry pancakes" and, after nine people had whispered around the table, we ended up with "pineap-ple tables." What?!

We live under the illusion that we *control* information. We believe that if we say exactly the right thing, people will understand what we mean and they will be committed to it. We craft messages and think about specific words because we make the assumption that if we can capture exactly the *right* words that will take care of engaging our people.

The fact is that we *don't* control information.

Imagine how the game of telephone plays out when you have a company of 300 people, or 800 people or 8,000 people. Even when you say it out loud instead of whispering it in the next person's ear, and even when you repeat it multiple times, you still get "pineapple tables."

Every individual is the center of his or her own universe. We bring our own history, experiences, personality, and perspectives to the world... *every time.* There's no escaping it. This is why we don't control information. People will take the information we provide—no matter how clearly we think we've communicated it or how carefully we've crafted the message—and they will add their own experiences and perspectives (based on their own personal stories) and make sense of it in their own way. They will do this *every time.*

What if we change how we think about information? Rather than considering it our role as leaders to provide information in ways that will inform and create "buy-in," what if we consider it our role to provide information that is meaningful and useful to people?

What if we trust people to make sense of the information we provide because they know their jobs and we have a strong organizational or team purpose? What if we actually provide time and space for people to interpret and make sense of the information we provide? What if we don't just provide instruction, but enable people to *Engage* with information, and with each other, in ways that create opportunities to find meaning?

SHARED MEANING

Here's an example of shared meaning. The annual goal of one division of a company was increased from $250M to $400M. That division needed to take on the increase because dynamics in the market were putting downward pressure on other divisions, making this increase necessary for the health of the company as a whole. It was an enormous leap, and the leaders of the division were anxious about announcing it to their people, who were already feeling overwhelmed.

The leaders spent time thinking about how to perfectly craft their message. Who should deliver it? How? What could they say about this complicated issue that would result in "buy-in" for the new goal?

One of the leaders on the team—notably, in the third layer down in the organizational chart—suggested that they host meetings, in small groups, with the managers who would be responsible for leading their teams through this challenge. What if they provided an opportunity to figure out together how this would impact the work and how they might engage their people in understanding and committing to the new goal?

No longer was an individual person—the *leader*—or a small group of leaders responsible for crafting a message to make this challenge okay for everyone. *It was not one person's responsibility.* The leaders decided to share the information openly and invite people to make sense of it together.

So they hosted conversations with key leaders throughout the division—in small groups, so that people could engage in the kind of give-and-take and dialogue that moves people toward real understanding. Through that engagement, each of the managers gained a deeper understanding of what they were being asked to do, why it was happening, and why it was so important for the company. They were able to figure out what about it was meaningful *for them*.

With that deeper understanding and sense of meaning, the managers were able to move beyond "buy-in" to real commitment, which enabled them to lead in their own ways, with their own teams. Building commitment among their teams also enabled everyone—managers and individual contributors alike—to own the success of that tremendous goal.

You may be thinking, *Yeah, but that process takes too much time.* In fact, the small group of leaders at the top probably would have spent comparable time slaving over exactly the right language to use that would motivate people to support the goal. Engaging people actually saved tremendous time throughout the process, as people were able to get down to work, make their own decisions, and take action based on their own deep understanding of what they were trying to accomplish together—just like that team on the field or the jazz band performing.

I'm happy to report that they achieved this huge goal. Not only did they celebrate achieving their goal, they celebrated the tremendous sense of accomplishment, teamwork, and commitment they had built together through the process.

Leading for engagement means actively seeking the kind of understanding that leads to commitment, instead of trying to find the right words to get "buy-in."

And the parking lot mafia? We'll visit them again in the third tool in *Engage*—Supporting the Counter-Narrative.

THE CEO SECRET FOR *ENGAGE*

Leadership is happening all the time, at all levels.

People who are engaged bring their best to every game... and they win.

As the CEO, you're the coach, not the quarterback.

TOOL 1:
LEAD FOR COMMITMENT

Look for opportunities to make sense of the work together. *Expect* that people will interpret the information you give them, based on their own personal stories and experiences.

When I was growing up, it seemed to me that my mom was always saying, "Because I said so, that's why. When you're the mom you can decide." Did your mom ever say that to you? I *hated* that. And, frankly, I only made a half-hearted effort to do what she asked when her explanation was only, "Because I said so."

When we're engaged, when we're committed to and care about what we're doing, we understand *why* we're doing it— it makes sense to the person asking us to do it and it makes sense to us. When that happens, things get done with conviction, perhaps even joyfully. There is context. When there's context, I can find a way to attach meaning to it for myself.

"Because I told you so" isn't engaging. (It's efficient, and sometimes it's necessary, but it's not engaging.) I would argue that, "This is a really important initiative and I feel confident that we're up to the challenge," is a little like saying, "I told you so," because it doesn't offer any space for interpretation, for taking the information and making sense of it as an individual.

"We do not exist at the whim of information; this is not the fearsome prospect which greets us in a world ravenous for information. Our own capacity for meaning-making plays a crucial role. We, alone and in groups, serve as interpreters, deciding which information to pay attention to, which to suppress."
–Margaret Wheatley, *Leadership and the New Science*

The leader can and should offer ideas about how something is meaningful: "We need to expand into this market to beat our competition" or "This initiative will increase our standing with customers" or "This new product gives us the leverage we need to grow." All of those messages are important and they convey that there are specific decisions that have been made on behalf of the organization.

And, still, each person will bring his or her own stories and experiences to their interpretation of those messages.

We have to understand in order to commit and that means we have to bring our own personal experiences to whatever information or ideas are shared. Acknowledging this opens up possibilities to *Engage* in new ways that give people opportunities to understand and be committed, not to just "buy in."

TOOL 2:
SEEK TO UNDERSTAND

The most prevalent way we communicate is to advocate for our position, to make the case for our own point of view—to argue for the things we *know*. When we're trying to *Engage*, when we're making the shift from knowing to understanding, we need to be equally committed to understanding others' points of view. This is a lesser practiced form of communication called *inquiry*. Inquiry is about trying to understand the other person's point of view.

Both advocacy *and* inquiry are important.

As we move from knowing to understanding, our modes

of communication shift. When we aren't striving to *know* (and to have everyone else think we know), we begin to ask more questions. When we're not taking the position of advocating for the answer that we know is right, we can more readily take the position of seeking to understand another person's experience or point of view.

Advocacy—pushing for our point of view or opinion—is the most common form of communication. It's what we're taught, and it's gotten us far in our careers. Being persuasive, presenting well, being the *expert*, has been useful as we moved up in the organization.

Now, though, when you're looking for opportunities to *Engage* your people, shifting from knowing to understanding, inquiry becomes equally—and sometimes more—valuable. Asking thoughtful questions about what brought a person to a particular position or what experiences they've had that informed their opinion opens up opportunities to find common ground and to inform current and future decisions and actions.

This is not to say that we stop advocating for our ideas and opinions altogether. Using advocacy and inquiry together expands our capacity for understanding and builds relationships in ways that are authentic and lasting.

The easiest way to expand your communication to include more inquiry is to ask more questions. Not "why" questions like, "Why did you do this that way?" Ask questions that start with phrases like, "Tell me more about..." or "I'm curious about..." or "Can you tell me about your thinking around that?" Those kinds of questions demonstrate your focus on inquiry and reflect your sincere interest in understanding.

The other important aspect of inquiry is, of course, listening. (Remember that listening is a tool from the first practice, *Embark*.) Asking questions but not listening to the answers is counter-productive. Not listening, especially after you've asked the question, will cause people to disengage faster than just about anything else.

There's more information about inquiry and advocacy in the Tool Kit at FindingTimeToLead.com.

TOOL 3:
SUPPORT THE COUNTER-NARRATIVE

The rumor mill is real. Rather than think about what you can say that will make the negative narratives disappear, try focusing on a strong counter-narrative so that people who don't want to be involved in the negativity can find the courage to shut it down.

Remember the parking lot mafia, the group that was busy weaving a narrative that the school principal was unfriendly and inaccessible? There were also parents who had had great interactions with the principal. Where were they when the parking lot mafia was telling everyone that the principal was unfriendly and inaccessible? They weren't brave enough to share their experiences, because the prevailing negative narrative was too strong. There wasn't an adequate counter-narrative for them to hold onto.

There were parents who could have said to the parking lot mafia, "Hmm. That's funny, I've had great interactions with her" or "I've found her to be very friendly and accessible" or "She's really busy, but I made an appointment and we had a great conversation. She even followed up with me a couple of times to see how my daughter is doing since we talked."

We *know* there are people who are not having the experience that is the fodder for the negative water cooler conversations. Where are they when we need them?

To tackle our parking lot mafia at the school, we switched our point of view. Rather than focus on what we could do to influence the group that was reinforcing the narrative that the principal was unfriendly and inaccessible, we focused on the people who might step up and provide a counter-narrative. What would it take for them to step up? How could we support them?

The people who had had a different experience needed to have a strong foothold that would support their different experience. In order to give them that foothold, the school principal pushed herself to be visible at drop-off time and to interact with parents—not specifically because she wanted to disprove the story that those parents were telling about her (although it was helpful for that), but because she wanted to support the parents who might be willing to share a counter-narrative, who might find the courage to step up with a different story if they saw her out there. She was actively helping them feel confident enough in their own experience to bravely cut off the prevailing narrative about how she was unfriendly and inaccessible.

We could have taken another approach. The principal could have hidden out in her office and allowed the parking lot mafia to control the narrative. I have seen individuals and organizations take that path. In one situation, the leader withdrew in the face of a prevailing narrative that he withheld information and didn't engage with people. He stopped interacting and stopped sharing information for fear of what "they" would do with the information he provided. He completely lived into the prevailing narrative that he withheld information. The people who wanted a more positive narrative got tired and left. Eventually, he was demoted from his position.

We do this. We simply stop sharing information because we're afraid of how it might explode on the rumor mill. Our fear of the parking lot mafia influences our decisions to the point that we second-guess everything and end up doing nothing.

We're so held hostage by the negative that we fail to support those who want a different narrative; those who, if given a modest level of support, would promote that counter-narrative for and with us.

Rather than withhold information or duck a particular situation or decision in order to minimize the response of those who might be negative, switch your point of view. Think about how you can support those who want to be positive.

(I guarantee they're out there.) Help them build a counter-narrative that expands their courage to step forward. Not only is that more productive, it's *way* more fun to think about how to support the positive people than it is to spend time thinking about how to avoid the negative.

* * *

When we communicate through both inquiry and advocacy, listen well, and support the counter-narrative, we *Engage* people in ways that are meaningful and productive.

Sharing information with the *expectation* that people will take that information and make sense of it for themselves opens possibilities for engagement that don't exist when we labor under the illusion that we control information and that if we just say the exact right thing people will understand and be committed.

PART THREE

— THE THIRD SHIFT —
FROM REACTING TO RESPONDING

Moving from reacting to responding gives us a wider perspective from which to thoughtfully make choices about who we'll be as a leader.

The two practices that support you in the shift from reacting to responding are *Encourage* and *Evolve,* which we'll explore in the next two chapters.

CHAPTER 5

ENCOURAGE

You know you're making the shift from doing to being, from knowing to understanding, and from reacting to responding when you start to look around and see potential in everyone around you. Seeing the potential in others, seeing the great things you could accomplish together, requires a certain distance, a perspective that isn't available when you're only reacting to the things around you. That potential you see comes forward if you are able to actively *Encourage* it.

A GLIMPSE OF GREATNESS

We have reorganized, reworked, reassigned, and retooled people and organizations to death. We've squeezed every last ounce of fat out of our layers. We've consolidated jobs and mechanized processes to the point of exhaustion. There's nothing left. There's no other place to cut; there are no more jobs to combine; and there is definitely no less work to do.

If that's the case, then maximizing the potential in our people is our last great competitive advantage. Not only that, it's the right thing to do.

People who feel like they have the opportunity to learn, grow, and contribute, will enthusiastically come to work, and they will *stay*, even when the going gets rough.

Enabling people to bring their best selves to their work, inviting them to make a contribution, and encouraging them to show up beyond what they thought was possible— that's how you bring greatness forward. That's your job.

I worked with a woman for many years who was internationally renowned for creating a methodology for teaching children. She was formidable—brilliant, driven and caring in her own way.

My first encounter with her was when I was a consultant for her organization. We had an hour-long one-on-one meeting that I didn't think went at all well and over the course of the project, I had a couple of additional short interactions with her. The project ended and I didn't see her or hear from her again until *five years later*, when she called me.

"Leslie, this is Maria. I'm starting a new organization and I could use your help. Could you meet with me this afternoon?"

Yep. Just like that. Out of the blue.

Over the course of the next nearly ten years that we worked together, I watched Maria do this countless times. She would have a (sometimes brief) interaction with someone during which she would glimpse greatness in them. She would file their name and what she saw in them away in the back of her mind and then, when an opportunity presented itself, she would call them and ask them to join her in her work. It was a great strategy in a small field where competition for talent was fierce.

Those of us who joined her worked hard, because we knew that she believed in us. We knew that working with her was an opportunity to stretch ourselves, to maximize our potential, and we jumped at the chance.

She saw greatness in us—often before we saw it in ourselves.

THE HERO'S JOURNEY

American mythologist, writer, and lecturer Joseph Campbell found that every story that has survived throughout human history has the same elements. He called this human story "The Hero's Journey."

Consider some of your favorite books or stories or movies. Think about some of the stories that are popular in our culture or that have endured over time—*Harry Potter, Star Wars*, great biographies, epic poems like *The Odyssey*. They all follow the same basic story arc: A hero receives a call and ventures forth from his or her normal circumstances—usually after a tragedy has occurred that propels the hero forward. Our hero struggles along the way, until a mentor steps in to teach and to help the hero claim his or her own gifts. From there, the hero ventures out further and, eventually, a great battle is won. After having fought additional forces of darkness in order to get home, our hero returns from the adventure with a treasure, or with the treasure of a new identity.

Think about Luke Skywalker in *Star Wars*, Frodo Baggins in *The Hobbit*, Katniss Everdeen in *The Hunger Games*—any of your favorite sport or superhero stories, and even the epic, award-winning hip-hop musical, *Hamilton*. Our favorite stories are about ordinary people who overcome obstacles on their way to fulfilling their destiny.

This became a more conscious formula for successful movies in 1985, when a memo that took Campbell's work and applied it to making movies was circulated in Hollywood. (If you'd like to learn more about the hero's journey, there is more information about it on our website: FindingTimeToLead.com.)

In the hero's journey, our hero always struggles. They face a loss of faith in themselves until a mentor appears to teach them and, more importantly, to *believe* in them, before they believe in themselves.

The mentor doesn't make it easy for the hero. On the contrary, the mentor pushes him, because the mentor expects greatness from the hero. The focus of the story is *always* on the hero and the mentor's actions always come from a place of *true service* to the hero. Often, the mentor makes a great sacrifice on behalf of the hero. The hero doesn't find the treasure and bring it back without the mentor's guidance, but the focus is never primarily on the mentor and what he or she can accomplish.

The role of the mentor is a key element in our very human story. Being a mentor is an incredible position from which to make a very real difference.

When you become a CEO, or any kind of leader, you are still on your own hero's journey, but you are no longer *only* the hero. Your own hero's journey continues, but the people in your company see you as the mentor.

If you want to unleash the potential in your people and take advantage of the last great competitive advantage, your most important role is that of mentor—whether you're the 24-year-old founder of a start-up or the 53-year-old CEO of a manufacturing company.

Being a mentor requires a shift from reacting to responding. When we're acting only as the hero in our own story, our reactions are more likely to be limited by our own perspective. We come from a place of *What should I do right now to support my own hero's journey?*

By contrast, if you're thinking of yourself as the mentor, you'll recognize the importance of *responding*.

You'll take a deep breath, count to ten, and picture this other person on their own hero's journey. How can you, as their mentor, teach them, support them, and build their confidence? How can you provide the kind of guidance that will lead them to success? What wisdom can you help them discover in themselves?

THE WISDOM IS IN THE ROOM

We were not raised or educated with the perspective that "the wisdom is in the room." Unless you went to a very different kind of school (of which there are a few), I'll bet that the vast majority of classrooms in which you were educated positioned the teacher in the front of the room, facing rows of desks or tables.

In large college classrooms, the teacher or professor is so much the focal point that the seats radiate out from the front on elevated risers, making it virtually impossible to engage with anyone but the person on either side of you.

This is often how we conceptualize leadership. The leader is like the teacher in that classroom. The knowledge, the wisdom, resides with him or her. No wonder we struggle to engage people! The sum total of our experience with how knowledge and wisdom get shared is often that we ask the teacher a question and he or she gives us the answer. If we operate from that perspective, it shouldn't surprise us that people feel disengaged from their own wisdom.

If you're going to fully embrace the mentor role, you'll need to challenge this vision of the leader as the keeper of wisdom. If you truly believe that "the wisdom is in the room," you invite others into the conversation with a gut-level assumption that you can and will learn from everyone; that the best answers are created by the *collective* wisdom in the room.

I recently learned this the hard way. Remember my propensity for hyper-responsibility? Well, I have to admit that sometimes it moves past thinking that I have to do everything and borders on thinking that no one else can contribute.

I was struggling to come up with a good training exercise to get my participants to experience using different perspectives. I was literally standing by myself in our training room staring off into space when one of my colleagues came in and said, "Can I help you with something?" To which I replied, "No, I'm just trying to think of an exercise for tomorrow."

Did you catch that? "*No*, I'm just trying to think of an exercise for tomorrow." I may as well have said, "No, I don't need or want your help. I'm struggling with something and I'm on a tight deadline, but your contribution wouldn't be useful right now." *Oops.*

I was reacting from my own immediate need to get something done and forgot (temporarily) that the wisdom was in the room.

Luckily, my team knows to keep asking questions. "Hmm. What are you trying to do with the exercise?" my colleague asked.

"I'm trying to get them to experience using different perspectives. Here's what I've got, but I don't think it works."

Then another colleague wandered into the room (because we can't resist conversations like these) and asked if he could help.

Pretty soon, the three of us were offering different ideas and thoughts—until we had the perfect solution. It took about ten minutes. (I'm pretty sure I had already been staring off into space for *at least* that long.)

My point is that it isn't easy or necessarily natural for us to truly embrace the idea that the wisdom is in the room. This is especially tough for those of us who are high-achieving and confident enough to become leaders in the hierarchical structure. We're pretty sure we have it figured out. But if we are always—consciously or unconsciously—picturing that classroom, we're not tapping into the wisdom that's in the room.

MENTOR AS STARRING ROLE

We have a colleague who, at one time in her career, had been responsible for a number of sales teams in a large consumer goods company. I'll call her Ann. Ann inherited teams that had been under a very command-and-control model of leadership. "The wisdom is in the room" was definitely *not* a prevailing philosophy. No one was willing to do anything they hadn't been explicitly asked to do. Fear ruled.

As her teams were downsized and competition in the industry got more fierce, Ann was faced with needing to do more with less. (Sound familiar?) She realized that the only way to get all of the work done was to have people show up differently. She needed them to take more initiative and to own more responsibility for the work of the team.

In short, Ann saw great potential in each individual and in

the team as a whole and knew she needed to tap into that potential. She saw the wisdom in the room and shifted the lens to think of herself as the mentor.

How could she tap into the potential she saw in her people? How could she get around the fear that was engrained in the culture of the team?

Ann realized that people needed to be *invited* to share their ideas and talents. She needed to *Encourage* them to step into a new way of operating. She needed to let her people know the greatness she saw in them. So she started to extend invitations to people to share the specific skill or perspective she saw in them with the team.

"Barry, I noticed that you're really great with spreadsheets. Could you create a template for the team?" or "Kiera, your graphs are very informative. Could I give you about ten minutes in our next meeting to show them to the team and talk about how they're helpful to you?"

Over time, the invitations became more general. "Linda, would you make a presentation at our quarterly sales meeting about how you're building relationships with clients? I'd be happy to talk it through with you a couple weeks before the meeting."

Eventually, people began asking Ann if they could have five minutes to report on an important team strategy or something new they'd tried. They began asking each other for information and support. They started stepping up and operating differently. They began sharing more of their wisdom with each other. They began *leading* themselves.

Ann had tapped into their individual and collective potential and that had exponential benefits for each person and for the team. Ann enjoyed being able, as the mentor, to move people forward on their own heroes' journeys.

When we can respond instead of react, we can change our point of view. We can see that the wisdom is in the room and we can *Encourage* it to come forward, on behalf of each individual, who is on their own hero's journey, and on behalf of the team.

THE CEO SECRET FOR *ENCOURAGE*

As leaders, we are called to intentionally consider our dual roles as hero in our own journey *and* as a mentor to others in their journey.

It is from the role of mentor that some of our proudest moments will come.

TOOL 1:
BE THE MENTOR

Adopt the perspective, the identity, of mentor and you will naturally respond in ways that bring out the best in others.

Think back to exploring your own personal story in Chapter 2. When you consider the peak experiences that moved you forward or that catapulted you to a new place or perspective, who was there to help make that happen? Who believed in you before you believed in yourself? Who pushed you past what you thought was possible?

A mentor doesn't have to be a boss. It could be a teacher, professor, coach, friend, colleague, parent or grandparent, minister or rabbi, spouse or partner. We're all mentors to each other in many ways.

When you ask yourself, *Who do I want to be in this moment?* do you think of one of those mentors? I would bet the answer is yes.

Sometimes, when I talk about mentors, people freak out and get overwhelmed by the thought of having to build a mentoring program. *This is not that.* Although formal mentoring programs can be very helpful and productive, especially when addressing issues of equity based on gender or race, they can also be overwhelming and those relationships can become forced.

What I'm talking about here is the idea of mentor as an attitude, an approach, an identity; the mentor whose focus is on the hero, not on him or herself; the mentor who makes sacrifices on behalf of the hero.

It's also important to note that being a mentor doesn't mean you have to be in a one-on-one, long-term relationship with an official "mentee."

A mentor may be with us for a long time, or mentoring may happen in a swift encounter that somehow nudges us back onto our own path.

When we adopt *mentor* as an identity, we can naturally seize opportunities to respond in a way that will *Encourage* those around us to fulfill their own destinies.

TOOL 2:
FIND YOUR "COME FROM" PLACE

Getting clear about where we're coming from in a given interaction or situation gives us a strong platform from which to deliver our message.

Have you ever heard someone say, "I don't get where he's coming from about that." Or when someone has an outburst you might hear yourself say, "Where did *that* come from?"

We really do have "come from" places.

What we say and do is rooted in those "come from" places— deep places that reflect our history or our life experiences, our mood in this moment, and our attitude toward this situation.

Knowing where we're "coming from" on an issue or topic helps to align our language with our tone and our body language, which makes everything we say more impactful.

I'll give you an example. I was on a call with a leader who needed to have a very difficult performance conversation with a direct report. She felt like it was important to the team dynamic and for the evolution of her organization that this person stay on the team, but his performance had been far below satisfactory.

She was really struggling with what to say to him. Should she give him the direct feedback and direction that she hoped would improve his performance? Or should she just let him go, in spite of the team's need for his skills? There were two distinct choices.

When you're really struggling with what to say, it usually means you're not clear about your "come from" place. Was she going to come from a place of hopefulness about his ability to improve his performance? Or a belief that she should fire him?

She was prepared to be clear with him about how he needed to change his behavior and how she would hold him accountable, but if she delivered that message from a place of not really believing he could do it, her words would be hollow. He wouldn't improve his performance if she wasn't coming from a place of believing that he could.

I asked her to take a deep breath. And then another. (Remember that this is one way to gain deeper access to the thinking part of the brain.)

Then I said, "I want you to answer this question immediately—do not stop to think about it. Here it is: Do you believe he can do this job?"

She responded, "I do think he can do this job." ("I do think" was a bit of a hedge, but I let her get away with it.)

"Okay," I said. "Then what do you want to tell him?"

From there, she was able to craft a message that conveyed both her deep concern and her belief that he could do the job if he changed his behaviors and took responsibility for that change.

But what if she had answered my question with, "No, I don't believe he can do this job"?

Then we would have crafted the message that he was being fired.

There is absolutely no point in saying something you don't really believe. It's confusing. And, by the way, people can see right through it. We get more than 50% (some estimates are as high as 70%) of any communication through a person's body language. Our body language *can't* lie.

Picture a time you had to tell someone something that you didn't really believe. Do you remember how uncomfortable that was? My shoulders go up and I get a lump in my throat. I can feel my eyes darting back and forth. I just *know* that I'm not going to be effective. If I don't believe what I'm saying, why should the person I'm talking to believe what I'm saying?

Getting clear about your "come from" place aligns your body language with your words and tone. You'll be amazed, as you practice this, how much more confidently you'll be able to deliver messages (especially tough messages) when you have identified that place clearly.

Look for a "come from" place that gives you confidence. Clear and genuine "come from" places of caring—about the person, the team, the customer, the goal, or the value—are powerful foundations for real conversation.

This isn't necessarily easy. Finding a positive "come from" place when you're angry or frustrated can be incredibly challenging. To help yourself, in that situation, you can ask yourself questions such as these:

- What is making me uncomfortable about this situation or conversation?
- What do I really believe about this situation?
- What do I care about here?
- Can I get to a positive "come from" place in this situation?
- How can I demonstrate my genuine care for this person?

You'll know when you've found a genuine place from which you can deliver a potentially challenging message. Something will shift in your body. For me, something settles in my abdomen, just under my belly button. I take a deep breath and instantly feel more calm and prepared. The words I want to use become clear.

Of course, I can't predict how the other person will respond, but when I have a sense of my own presence in the conversation, I feel like I can be who I want to be and I feel like what I have to say will be delivered with clarity and confidence.

Finding a genuine, caring "come from" place from which to deliver a message that is aligned with what you really believe... that's a powerful tool. Delivering a message with clarity and confidence is *especially* important in the role of mentor. If you'd like more information about finding your "come from" place, you'll find it in the Tool Kit on our website: FindingTimeToLead.com.

TOOL 3:
TELL THE TRUTH

We *Encourage* others when we tell the truth. Effective mentoring comes from a place of doing what is best for the hero, even when it's difficult.

In the television show *Game of Thrones*, Jon Snow, the hero, struggles to find the courage to pursue his destiny. He and one of his mentors, Sir Davos, have the following exchange.

Sir Davos: "You go on and you fight for as long as you can. You clean up as much of their shit as you can."

Jon Snow: "I don't know how to do that. I thought I did. I failed."

Sir Davos: "Good. Now go fail again."

Sir Davos doesn't sugarcoat the situation. He doesn't give Jon Snow some platitude about how things will get better. He tells him the truth.

That is easier said than done. It's easy to claim busy-ness in order to dodge the hard conversations. It may seem like it saves time to take a pass from delivering the difficult news. But when we're really being the mentor, when we're responding instead of reacting, we tell the truth.

> *"Leadership is not a rank worn on a collar. It is a responsibility that hinges almost entirely on character. Leadership is about integrity, honesty and accountability. All components of trust. Leadership comes from telling us not what we want to hear, but rather what we need to hear. To be a true leader, to engender deep trust and loyalty, starts with telling the truth."*
> –Simon Sinek, *Leaders Eat Last*

Telling the truth means providing real, meaningful recognition and praise *and* providing real, meaningful criticism.

The mentor comes from a place of *true belief* in the hero. From that place, the mentor can offer the praise and criticism that enables the hero to fulfill his or her destiny. When we don't get tripped up by our own role as hero, we don't have to take time second-guessing our response.

Telling the truth from the perspective of the mentor draws out that latent potential that is our last, greatest competitive advantage. (And it's the right thing to do.)

* * *

When we move from reacting to responding, we're able to *Encourage* others in ways that unleash their potential. We take on the role of mentor, come from a place of genuine care, and naturally invest in others' capacity to fulfill their own destinies.

CHAPTER 6

EVOLVE

The CEO you are today isn't the CEO you will be in a year or a decade or even next week. You're continually growing into the CEO you hope to be. That forward motion is accelerated if you're able to consciously respond to the people and situations around you that are calling you to *Evolve*.

"The person I am at any given moment is neither identical to the persons of other moments nor to the larger identity which is supposed to endure through the sum of moments."
~ Robert Grudin, *Time and the Art of Living*

It's true that we show up differently in every moment, depending on the situation, the people, the relationships, our mood, and our current perspective. It's also true that we have a larger identity that "endures through the sum of moments."

We carry our life experiences, our stories, our perspectives, and the best and worst of who we've been before into every new situation.

Evolution is a complex and variable process and it only happens over time. The more aware we can be of the experiences and challenges around us and who they are calling us to be, the more intentional we can be about our efforts to *Evolve*.

LEADERSHIP IS NOT A DESTINATION

I recently met with a woman, Meredith, who runs her own company. The company has grown over the past five years from only herself and a partner to more than 30 people. This growth has dramatically changed the demands of her job.

Meredith used to spend the majority of her time building and nurturing deep relationships with clients. She loves that aspect of her job. Her unique skill in that area is responsible, in no small measure, for the growth of her company.

Over time, she's also built a strong reputation in her industry. She's being called to serve on boards and committees that could have a meaningful impact on her entire industry.

Meanwhile, her children are leaving for college and her father has become quite ill, requiring more of her personal time and attention.

Meredith is at an edge, a moment that requires her to show up differently in all areas of her life. There are people and situations demanding different things from her and she will have to *Evolve* to meet those needs.

The demand to *Evolve* is especially urgent in a growing company. In the early days of a company, decisions can be made in conversations in the hallway between two or three people. Those decisions can be communicated out quickly, and you can count on bumping into just about everyone you might need to inform or update about that decision over a short time span. This isn't the case as the company gets bigger.

If your company is growing, you may no longer know everyone. The company may now have people all over the globe. Even if you're in a small company that has grown from one or two people to ten or fifteen, that's still exponential growth that requires the leader to evolve.

Human organizations are living systems. They are never static. Whether we're leading a fast-growing company, a start-up, or a mature company in a mature industry, things are changing. New realities are constantly calling on us to *Evolve*. How do we tune in to those demands and be intentional about our own growth and evolution?

REFLECTION

We are not always trained to really *look* at things. How often do we reflect on our experiences or think about what those experiences mean for us? How often do we take the time to acknowledge the inputs that might be calling us to *Evolve*?

Take a minute right now to observe yourself in your role as CEO. What do you see? Reflect for a minute on what you've learned as CEO. Can you pinpoint a few moments or situations where major learning occurred? What did you do in response? How did that change you? Think about this from a perspective of being exactly in that moment, and of going forward over a longer time frame. Are there repeating experiences that might be calling you to try something new?

There's a term from cultural anthropology research that is useful for thinking about reflection: "participant observer." As a participant observer, the researcher is a full participant in the day-to-day interactions of the culture and *simultaneously* distant enough to see it objectively and to discern the patterns through which the culture expresses itself.

This is what it looks like to really practice reflection. You can be both *in* the situation and also observing it and looking for the learning opportunities. This perspective requires self-awareness, self-discipline, and the ability to be both in the situation *and* outside of it. Not an easy task.

The best example I can think of is when I'm facilitating a meeting or training. When I'm at the front of the room, I have to be aware of many things simultaneously. I'm watching for the reactions of participants. *Are they getting it? Are they falling asleep? Are they secretly looking at their phones under the table?* (By the way, we always know.) *How do I need to adjust right now to accommodate those inputs?* I'm participating fully in what's going on.

And I'm observing how I am in that space right then. *Am I really in this or am I thinking about my next meeting or what we're having for lunch? How am I holding the space? What is the energy I'm adding to the room?*

And I'm thinking about larger implications of what I'm doing right then. *Did we prepare adequately? Should we have done something differently with the slides or the hand-outs? Does this section need to be longer or shorter?*

I'm participating in the training, taking questions, covering content, facilitating conversations, and I'm *simultaneously* aware of myself in the situation and thinking about how all of what's happening plays into the larger scheme of things.

That awareness—my ability to be both participant and observer—enables me to deeply look at what's going on and to make adjustments, both in the moment and over the longer term.

Sometimes it's impossible to be even modestly objective. For conversations that start with, "Am I crazy ...?" we may need to invite someone else to look at something with us or for us. We need to see the reflection of the situation—and of ourselves—in another person's eyes.

LONELY AT THE TOP

"Lonely at the top" is real.

There are issues and decisions you face as CEO that you aren't able to discuss with anyone in your company. Tough personnel decisions, external challenges to the business, your own internal struggles. These types of issues affect those around you in ways that make sharing your thoughts with them impossible.

Identifying a person or group of people to whom you can turn when you need to talk through things will save you time and headaches. We all need that person who will give us the look that says, "You know what you need to do here; you're just avoiding it." It's the kick in the ass we need, especially when things are challenging.

Having a coach or mentor who will remind you of your own highest aspirations as a CEO, especially when it's hard, can accelerate your evolution toward being the kind of leader you hope to be.

Equally important are the friends, family, spouse or partner—the community that supports you and from which you draw strength. It's crucial to make time for them. They are, many times, your most important reflection partners, because they know your particular "persons of other moments," your different roles and your personal story.

They can help you connect with the long-term view that's required for you to *Evolve*.

HONORING TIME

The first step in this whole process was *Embark*. Remember? I asked you to make a choice. I asked you to choose to *Embark* on a journey, not because you want to get quickly to a definite destination, but because you recognize this is a path and because you want to accelerate your speed on that path by knowing where to put your attention.

CEO is who you *are*; it's not what you *do*. You don't have to *make* time for leadership; you just have to lead. Although you don't have to *make* time for leadership, expanding your relationship to time can be very helpful.

If being busy is *really* important to you, you may want to skip this section. If you're thinking, *It's not that being busy is* important *to me; it's just the reality of my life*, then you should definitely continue reading.

We can all get *hooked* on being busy. As the CEO, you're *supposed* to be incredibly busy. It's an expectation. I'm not trying to take that away from you. You *are* busy. No doubt. There's a lot to get done.

In fact, though, we do make *choices* about our time and how we spend it.

"We struggle with, agonize over and bluster heroically about the great questions of life when the answer to most of these lie hidden in our attitude toward the thousand minor details of each day."
~ Robert Grudin, *Time and the Art of Living*

We are controlled by our perceptions of time. This perception of uncontrollable busy-ness and lack of time gets reinforced every time we say, "I'm too busy" or "There's no time for that" or "I've gotten 52 emails while we've been sitting here." Our attitude toward time really is reflected in our "attitude toward the thousand minor details of each day."

Our perception of our *lack of control* over time gives us cover for making bad decisions, for taking shortcuts we know we shouldn't take, and for avoiding the real work that may be in front of us. We give in to the drive for short-term solutions, instead of investing in the long-term resolutions that could save us time in the long run.

Some things do take longer. Many of the things that matter take a long time. Evolution takes generations. Honoring time by paying attention to when things are really ripe for conversation, decision, or action actually *saves* time in the long run.

Think of the last time you rushed to make a decision or take action, even though you hadn't involved the people you needed to, or because you were feeling pressure from an outside source to present a solution. You probably said something like, "We're going with this decision because we don't have time to talk about it anymore."

Can you see how saying, "because I don't have time" implies that you're not responsible? When we say, "because I don't have time," it implies that the difficulty of the situation is somehow time's fault, not ours. Time becomes the excuse. But it is, in fact, your responsibility. If that decision or action doesn't go well, it's on you.

If time wasn't an easy excuse, if we really considered our attitudes toward the "thousand minor details of each day" and made decisions about how we spend our time, how might those decisions play out differently over the longer term?

Sometimes, yes, there are surprises and we don't have time to do what we'd like to do. And, absolutely, there are times when we do need to stop talking about things and make a decision. More often than not, though, we don't have time *now* because of a myriad of choices we made in the past about how we spent our time. And those decisions have led up to this moment.

What if we accept that we have more control over time than we thought we did, so that we can be bold in our decisions about how we spend our time? Then we move toward eliminating time as an excuse for poor decisions and reckless action.

AT THE EDGES

If we're truly evolving, adapting in response to new information and inputs, then we will necessarily come upon edges—places where we are pushed to move past our previous experiences. Becoming a CEO is a good example of coming up to an edge. It pushes you in new ways and into new territory.

Edges are exciting and often we seek them out. They are also stressful and challenging.

Dancing at a new edge means moving into uncertainty. We haven't been here before. What will it mean for us? Can we handle it? How can we manage time to make the best of this opportunity?

I personally get very cranky when I'm at a new edge. Seriously cranky. I don't like leaving the comfort of what I know I'm good at to move into something I haven't done before. For me to move past an edge there either needs to be a big push—which usually looks like trying to fulfill a need for a client that is something we haven't done before or fielding an idea from a colleague that I know makes sense, even though it will be hard (like writing this book). A big pull can also move me to an edge. That usually looks like an opportunity that is particularly enticing or exciting.

You'd think that when it's an exciting opportunity I wouldn't get cranky, but I still do. It's so bad that I usually have to apologize to my team. I just say outright, "I'm at a real edge with this project and it's making me very cranky. I'm sorry." (They dutifully say they can't tell, but I know they're just being nice.)

What happens for you when you're at an edge? I've seen CEOs who get aggressive when they're at an edge. They feel pressured and want to rush through the discomfort to get to the next place, which they hope will be more comfortable. They move quickly and sometimes snap at people who aren't keeping up. They talk about how they wish there was more time to do what they want to do, and lament that there's never enough time.

That rush usually ends up costing them a tremendous amount of time later, when they have to clean up the mess they've made. Or when they find themselves at the next edge and no one is there with them. Everyone else stayed behind because they were afraid of the unknown *and* afraid of their leader.

Some CEOs I've partnered with freeze when they come to an edge and can't make a move. They distract themselves by focusing on the minute details of each project or task. They avoid whatever fear or discomfort the edge is creating for them by putting their attention on things they can predict and control. They burn up time focusing on the wrong things and then, usually, end up having to make a snap decision because the circumstances catch up with them or because they finally realize that their people are standing around scratching their heads, wondering when their leader will make a move.

As a participant observer, you can be aware of your responses when you're at an edge. I usually notice my crankiness first and *then* recognize that I'm at an edge. Sometimes I know an edge is coming and, in an attempt to minimize my lizard-brain response, I try to think about how I'll prepare myself for the discomfort that comes with the approaching edge.

If you want to lead your company forward, innovate, move into new markets, build new products, create a new culture, you will have to *Evolve*—and there will be many edges. Evolution is a long process. When you take the long view, time is on your side.

How you handle your own edges, and how you navigate through the inevitable discomfort that accompanies them, will determine how the people in your company handle their edges. That, in turn, will determine your company's capacity for the new things you have in mind for building and growing your organization.

THE CEO SECRET FOR *EVOLVE*

Progress happens at the edge between where we've been and where we want to go.

When we reflect on what's going on around us, we're able to recognize when we're being called to *Evolve* in response to those edges. We can take responsibility for how we spend our time, and we can make decisions that enable us to intentionally *Evolve*.

TOOL 1:
DARE TO SAY "I DON'T KNOW"

Three simple words that can be helpful at the edges are "I don't know." Does that surprise you?

When you're leading others past what they've known and into uncertain territory, saying "I don't know" is sometimes the best and most efficient thing you can do. It acknowledges that you're in unknown territory and that not knowing is okay. Saying "I don't know"—especially when you're the CEO—also generously gives others the opportunity to share what they know, and to admit when they don't know.

When we're in new territory, we're not *supposed* to know. That's the point. We've left what we know and can predict behind in order to pursue something more interesting and exciting.

Saying "I don't know" gives others the opportunity to offer what they know by demonstrating your humility and your belief in the team. You're admitting that you cannot possibly know everything.

One of the CEOs I've worked with uses this phrase: "I think we've reached the end of my best offer." That's his signal that he has contributed what he can, for now, regarding his expertise and his role, to the current effort. He is signaling his threshold of "I don't know" and asking others on the team to step forward and contribute their knowledge and experience—their best offers—to move the project forward. This proactively encourages others to consider both the potential and the limits of what they bring to the table, and demonstrates the CEO's belief in the power of the team. It sends a message that we can survive in "I don't know."

If you're the CEO of a complex organization, never saying "I don't know" is pretending that it's possible for you to know everything there is to know about your people, your products, your company, and your industry. That not only undermines the knowledge and experience of those who really *do* know, it sets you up to spend time worrying about the humiliation you'll experience when they find out you really don't know.

TOOL 2:
STRENGTHEN YOUR REFLECTION MUSCLE

If we're going to adapt to the new challenges that we inevitably face as CEOs, we need to participate fully in everything around us and, *simultaneously*, manage ourselves, so that we can pick up on cues and clues that are calling us to *Evolve*.

The muscle to build is the one for reflection. There are many ways to build reflection into your day, and reflection can be built into what you're already doing.

A first, powerful way to invite more reflection is to create some small spaces for silence. I worked with the CFO of a large company who was driving home one night and ended up in a completely different place than her house. Has that ever happened to you? She was so distracted with a specific problem that her brain was trying to solve that she randomly drove to a location where she'd attended a meeting three days earlier. She described it as "kind of scary" that her brain could do that without her consciously thinking about it.

Since then, she has started using the time in her car for quiet reflection, not specific problem solving. She gets in her car and takes three deep breaths. She leaves the radio off and asks herself what happened during the day that she feels good about and what happened that she'd change if she could. Then she quietly lets her brain work on that while she drives home (instead of driving to some random place).

The deep breaths are important to help you reconnect with the thinking part of your brain and make a conscious choice to focus.

The CFO reports that what's really fascinating is that, often, while her brain is engaged in quiet reflection about her day, other parts of her brain are industriously working on that other big problem. Sometimes she gets home with the solution to something she'd been working on *and* her reflections about the day, along with some clear intentions for the next day.

So you can use your time in transit—in the car, on the train, on the bus, walking—to think about your day. It's that simple. Just remember to start with those three deep breaths.

Another built-in opportunity for reflection is at the end of meetings or conversations. Asking simple questions like "Did you get what you needed?" or "Do you feel like we made progress here?" can begin to train everyone's brain to reflect. When you ask those questions, other people ask themselves *Did I get what I needed? Do I feel like we made progress?*

With simple questions like these, you get the input you need to continue to *Evolve* and you build that muscle for reflection in everyone who interacts with you. It takes very little time to do this, and it builds a new level of productivity into your interactions.

Two options for building your muscles for reflection that do require you to use your time differently are journaling and meditation.

Let's start with journaling. We had an up-and-coming leader in one of our training programs who discovered the powerful effects of journaling when it was part of an exercise we did in the class. He decided that it was a very valuable tool for him and so set up a routine of journaling every morning with his first cup of coffee.

When I asked him to tell me about the value of journaling, he said, "In a single word: clarity. Journaling on a regular basis has offered me an opportunity to improve my self-awareness and get in tune with the running narrative in my head. This clarity has helped me collect my thoughts regarding complex or ongoing challenges. On a personal level, it has also helped me gain a better understanding of who I am, and think about how I want to show up each and every day."

Meditation is another practice that supports reflection and making the shift from reacting to responding. There are scientific studies that credit meditation with decreased blood pressure, improved alertness, and an increase in the brain's capacity to change—structurally and functionally.

You don't have to meditate 30 minutes every day in order to see benefits from meditation. Even turning your attention toward meditation for 30 *seconds* before you get out of bed can improve your brain's ability to focus. Meditation simply helps you be more aware of your unconscious thoughts and how they might be influencing how you operate in the world.

I find that when I actively pursue my meditation practice I'm vastly more efficient. I feel confident that I can get my brain to focus, I don't get distracted as easily, and I'm more creative.

There are many ways to build reflection into your daily routine. For more in-depth information about the practices I mention here—and other helpful practices, visit our website: FindingTimeToLead.com.

TOOL 3:
HONOR TIME

Evolution is an endless process. It's not done in an hour or a day or a week. It takes years, decades, centuries, millennia, forever. There are times of rapid growth and there are times for sitting still. Honoring time, paying attention to the ebb and flow of things, and taking responsibility for how we spend our time is critical if we're going to *Evolve* with intention.

Most of us seem to *like* our busy-ness. Many of us are addicted to it. Busy-ness makes us feel important and needed. If we want to truly *Evolve*, however, we need to shift our relationship to time. What if we accept—really accept—that we have a high level of control over our time? What if we take responsibility for how we spend time? We can recognize that we sometimes (often) use busy-ness as an excuse to get to a quick decision or action because we're uncomfortable in the space between what we know and what we can't yet know.

This space in between—the interim time—is perhaps the most important aspect of evolving. It's where the really juicy stuff happens. In complex systems, it's where the solutions get time to emerge. If we rush this in-between time because it's uncomfortable or if we avoid the discomfort altogether, we will miss important inputs and information. We will miss the opportunity to *Evolve* into the kind of person and CEO or the kind of organization that can successfully (and more efficiently) tackle the next edge. Often, when we short-circuit the interim time, the best solution eludes us.

My challenge to you is to let go of being busy for the sake of being busy, to actively shift your relationship with time and to stop thinking of it as something over which you have no control.

I recognize that that's not as easy as it sounds. Here's a simple beginning step: Shift your language. Whenever you find yourself saying or thinking things like, "I don't have time for that right now," try substituting "I'm choosing to do these things instead of that one." Rather than saying, "We don't have time for that," try saying, "We haven't left ourselves enough time for that." Try switching from, "That would be great, but we don't have time," to "That would be great. How can we build in time for that when we do this next time?"

When we talk about time as something we have a choice about, the locus of control shifts. Time is not in charge of us, like a tyrant to whom we must bow. We take control.

Simple shifts in language can create big shifts in our thinking. In turn, those shifts in our thinking can lead to big shifts in our culture.

* * *

Leadership requires us to *Evolve,* to take in the information and inputs all around us so we can respond to the challenges that are inevitably part of leading our companies to new edges. Daring to say "I don't know," building our muscle for reflection, honoring time, and always watching out for opportunities to learn support our capacity to *Evolve* into the type of leader we aspire to be.

CHAPTER 7

EXTEND

You're making the shift from doing to being, from knowing to understanding, and from reacting to responding. You aren't *making* time for leadership, you're *finding* time to lead, because you're showing up differently. You're *choosing* how you want to show up and who you want to be, in any given moment. Your best self is actively in the room at all times (well, *most* of the time).

Why is it so important that we show up as our best selves as often as possible? What makes this so essential?

It is because, as Wilfred Drath and Charles Palus explore in their article "Common Sense—Leadership as Meaning-Making in a Community of Practice," we are unique individuals who are simultaneously deeply embedded in social systems. How we show up influences the social systems we're in and *simultaneously* the systems influence who we are as unique individuals.

"When we act on what matters, on our own values, we support others in doing the same."
~ Peter Block

What do I mean by *system*? A social system could be a family, team, company, community, board of directors, organization, or classroom—any way we're engaged with others, especially when we're engaged over time.

If we show up as our *best* self, we are actively influencing the social systems we're part of for the better. If we don't, we are actively influencing the social systems for the worse (case in point: our parking lot mafia).

This is especially true for you as a CEO. Your span of influence is vast. As Simon Sinek says, "As the leader goes, so goes the culture."

This final practice, *Extend*, is about the importance of our choices about how we show up, and what we're willing to do to show up as our best selves.

WE'RE ALWAYS CHOOSING

Remember my friend Jim who would take forever to walk across campus because he interacted with so many people along the way? It was *always* true that Jim took time to reach out to people. It didn't matter how late he was or how frustrating it was for the people walking with him or waiting for him at his destination. It didn't matter if it was freezing cold outside or 100 degrees. It didn't matter that he had raging cancer, which he did. Walking across campus and talking to people along the way was Jim's *choice* about how he showed up on that campus, in that culture, and in the world. He made that choice every single day—and how he showed up made a difference every single day.

There were nearly 5,000 people at Jim's funeral service. We came from all over the world, each of us actively doing our best to show up in the ways that Jim had demonstrated for us. Students, faculty, and other administrators had been inspired by how he showed up, and so they did the same. Through Jim's example, the campus built an international reputation based on its caring and inclusive culture.

"The world is changed by your example, not by your opinion."
~ Paulo Coelho

I'm sure there were days when Jim wasn't perfectly "on." I'm sure there were days when it was hard to show up in those ways. I know there were days when he wasn't physically able to do what he wanted to do.

I also know that I could always count on Jim to be doing his best. He was always reaching into a reservoir, a zone of genius, where he was crystal clear about who he was and how we wanted to show up in the world.

We each have a reservoir, a zone of genius, and a place of crystal clear choice that we can tap into.

SO WHY CALL THIS *EXTEND*?

You may be thinking that *Extend* refers to extending our reach, expanding our influence. That is one reason that the seventh practice is called *Extend*. When you're operating as your best self and showing up consistently in the world that way, you absolutely *Extend* your reach and expand your influence. Jim's reach extended throughout campus, to other universities, around the world, and across generations of students and faculty.

This practice is also called *Extend* because, as leaders, we cannot stay in our own narrowly defined comfort zones. Leadership asks more of us. We are required to *Extend* ourselves beyond what we might personally think is useful or expected. We have to take everything in. In our quest to serve our people and our company, we will need to seek out different ideas, points of view, and experiences, so that we can relate to a broad spectrum of people, and so that we can see the larger patterns that may help us find a way forward.

But the main reason this last practice is called *Extend* is because of my favorite definition of love. In his 1978 book, *The Road Less Traveled*, M. Scott Peck defined love as "the will to extend oneself for the purpose of nurturing one's own and another's spiritual growth." My paraphrase of this is "Love is the will to extend yourself on behalf of another."

I believe that leadership, in its truest sense, is about love. Not an ooey, gooey, Valentine's Day kind of love. Leadership is about the kind of deep and compassionate love that connects us as human beings; the kind of love that sees potential and brings it forward; the kind of love that sits quietly with discomfort and bears witness through chaos; the kind of love that tells the truth because it's the kindest thing to do. That kind of love.

Love is the will to extend yourself on behalf of another.

It is not about changing who you are. It's not about "being nice." It's not about hearts or smiley faces or rainbows or unicorns. It's about simply exercising the will to extend ourselves on behalf of another.

EXERCISING OUR WILL

The *will* to extend is, for me, the critical piece of that definition of love. Extending ourselves on behalf of another is not necessarily an easy thing to do. It takes courage to push ourselves outside our comfort zones into the unknown and the uncertain because that is what another person needs from us. It's challenging to do things that we think are weird or dumb, but we do them anyway, because it's important to another person or because we know it will serve the larger group. It takes conviction to believe that it's worth it.

That *will* comes from *being*, not *doing*. It is accessible when we move past *knowing* and embrace *understanding*. It is made visible when we *respond* instead of *react*.

And, most importantly, it's a choice.

As a CEO, as a leader, it's up to you to pursue the practices that enable you to have the will and the capacity to extend yourself on behalf of others.

Leadership isn't something you do; it's someone you are.

Are you the person who has the will to *Extend* yourself on behalf of another?

What will it take for you to be that person?

DOING THE DISHES

My simplest example of this is about my husband. Dan is an incredibly gifted musician and composer. This means that 80% of the time at least 50% of his brain is occupied by music. He will pour milk into his coffee and leave the milk (and the coffee) on the counter for hours (or days), because the music occupying his brain distracted him.

When we first started living together, I was travelling a lot. I would leave the kitchen in great shape—dishes done, counters wiped off, food put away—you know the drill. I would come home three days later and the kitchen would be *trashed*. I knew, from having visited Dan when he lived alone, that it didn't bother him at all (at least not for a very long time). But it bothered me *a lot*.

After coming home to a trashed kitchen a few times, I told Dan that when the kitchen was a mess it really stressed me out and made me feel like he thought it was my job to clean the kitchen. I told him it felt like he didn't care that the messy kitchen bothered me.

You know what he does now? He *always* cleans the kitchen before I get home from a trip. I'm sure that while I'm away there are dishes stacked to the ceiling and food everywhere, because he absolutely doesn't care. But because he knows that a clean kitchen is important to me, and because he loves me, he's willing to *Extend* himself and clean up the kitchen (even though, to this day I don't think he has any idea why I think it's such a big deal).

Sometimes, extending ourselves on behalf of another is simple and easy—taking five minutes to walk to someone's cube or office instead of sending an email, because the message will be clearer in person; or asking how someone is doing, because it looks like they're having a rough day; or simply saying, "Thank you."

Sometimes, though, extending ourselves on behalf of another is not simple or easy. I worked with an executive who would literally avoid conflict at any cost. Anytime things got the least bit uncomfortable or people started disagreeing in the slightest, he would do or say something funny to break the tension and—he hoped—quickly move people along past the conflict.

It became clear, over time, however, that his team needed him to deal with conflict—as all teams do. They needed him to make decisions and stand by those decisions, even when it made people uncomfortable.

That executive has been working hard to *Extend* himself into that area of dealing with conflict instead of diverting it, even though it is truly painful for him. He's asked his boss and a couple of trusted colleagues to support him and to hold him accountable when he begins to shy away from what he needs to do around a conflict. Then he grits his teeth and stands his ground. It's hard work, but it's worth it because of the positive changes that result from doing what his team needs him to do.

The *Extend* practice is a challenge to tap into the reservoir that is the clearest version of our best selves so that we can muster the will to *Extend* ourselves on behalf of others.

THE CEO SECRET FOR *EXTEND*

Exercise your will. *Extend* yourself on behalf of others.

Show up—for yourself, for those you lead, for your company, for your family, for your community, and for our shared future.

TOOL 1:
TAKE IT ALL IN

Don't reject what you don't know or don't like just because it's unfamiliar or because you can't see how it fits. You *Extend* yourself when you look for meaning everywhere. When you make unexpected connections, you're able to think in metaphor and talk in stories.

There are all sorts of ways we can *Extend* ourselves and inspire our brains to see new things and make new connections. Change your scenery. Take a walk. Get out in nature. Go to the highest point and look around. Have a meeting at an unfamiliar coffee shop. Take your team on an overnight—out of town and away from the office. Visit another city. Talk to people outside your field. Do *anything* that is out of your daily grind. That distance, those new inputs, will trigger connections in your brain that wouldn't have come otherwise.

Something else that can re-calibrate your brain—and it works better than anything else I've found—is to engage in any kind of creative pursuit. Build something with Lego, go to an art museum, see a play, listen to music, play a video game with your son, attend a concert, watch a great movie, read fiction or poetry, spend time with small children. Those activities all force you into a different point of view. They activate different parts of your brain. They give you inputs that enrich your perspective.

You will return to your world with new ideas and new connections.

In my company, we intentionally weave artists throughout our leadership training. A composer presents about listening, composition, and how he decides when to solo, when to accompany, or when to play the bass line. He talks about what leadership looks like when you're leading a jazz band. We invite a poet to tell of the hero's journey of *The Odyssey*. She asks participants to reflect on their own hero's journey and she shares her poetry on the subject.

We build catapults, take walks together, and play games—all to get people into a different framework, to provide a different lens through which they can view themselves and their work.

We like to stretch leaders to think in metaphor, to make connections that seemed impossible before. That's how patterns emerge. That's how we begin to draw on past experiences and apply them in new ways—by actively seeking connections between the things we know and new experiences.

This is important for leaders because, as leaders, we are called to find meaning *everywhere*. We don't have the luxury of writing things off because they're unfamiliar or because we don't understand how they apply. It's our responsibility to be looking everywhere, to experience everything with an open mind and with open eyes, because we never know what experience those critical "ah-ha!" moments will emerge from. Nothing can be rejected out of hand.

The COO of a large company was in one of our "Music as Metaphor" sessions. She described herself as "not really a music person," but she challenged herself to be open to the learning. Later, she reported that she hadn't thought she'd gotten much out of the "Music as Metaphor" training—until she was talking with a colleague in her office and it occurred to her that the music metaphor would be the perfect vehicle for making something clear to that person.

As it turns out, it's more interesting and impactful to engage someone in a conversation about Miles Davis and how he doesn't always play solo than it is to tell someone that he's hogging all the attention and not letting his team demonstrate what they know. Taking in something completely new had expanded her capacity to connect with her colleague.

Take it all in. There are connections everywhere and they're yours to discover and leverage.

(There's a big list of things you can do to "take it all in" on our website at FindingTimeToLead.com.)

TOOL 2:
BELIEVE IN YOURSELF

Our belief in ourselves and in our gifts is where we find the courage to confidently act.

"To believe your own thought, to believe that what is true for you in your private heart, is true for all men, that is genius."
~ Ralph Waldo Emerson

There's so much that we can't know, but there are some things we can be sure of—things that we believe in so strongly that we can stand up for them in the face of resistance.

We recently brought together a group of our leadership program alumni for a "refresher." Thirty very busy executives were asked to give up four hours on a Friday afternoon before a three-day weekend. These are *busy* people who are quick to tell you how busy they are.

Suffice it to say that there was a *lot* of grumbling. Two different department heads told me that they'd gotten some pushback and people were asking if this was really necessary. The CEO asked me three times how many people were coming and if maybe we should cancel it because everyone was so busy.

It was really tempting for me to just cancel the training.

(I also had other places I could be for four hours on that Friday before a three-day weekend.) *If people aren't really into it, who am I to push them? Maybe I should just let them off the hook.*

And then I remembered how deeply I believe in what we teach and I thought about how powerful it is to get this group together. I reflected on how every time we've gotten them together they've commented on how glad they were that they made the time, how refreshed they were afterward, and how nourished they were by their time together.

I didn't know for sure how it would turn out, but I understood that they needed it. I got clear about how certain I am "in my private heart" that they would be enriched by spending the time together. From that foundation, I firmly and confidently held my ground.

Twenty-six of the thirty people arrived for the training, and I'm very confident that they told the people who weren't there that they missed out on something special.

In the end, we can't *know* the answers. We can't *know* what we will encounter on the way. We can't *know* that we will be successful. We can, however, *understand* that it's hard to make choices. We can *understand* that there are a thousand reasons not to do something. And we can *understand* that in the possibility of failure there is also incredible potential for learning.

We can understand, and then we can be sure. We can be certain "in our private heart" that we are headed in the right direction, that this is the right thing to try right now.

Think of a time when you had to really screw up your courage to stay true to what you believed "in your private heart." How would you describe what were you staying true to? What do you believe in so strongly that you'll stand up for it in spite of resistance?

When you're clear about *that*, everything else falls into place.

TOOL 3:
DO THE WORK

I wish I could say that I am perfect at doing and being all of the ways I talk about in this book. (Have you ever heard the phrase "We teach what we most need to learn?") I wish I could point to someone who has this all figured out and we could all focus on trying to be that person. But it doesn't work that way. This leadership stuff is work. It is a practice. Some days we're really on it and some days we're not at all.

Every day we get up in the morning with the intention of bringing our best self to our work. We operate from moment to moment with the will to extend ourselves on behalf of others. But, even with this great intention, our lizard brain is constantly putting up resistance, reminding us of potential dangers and wanting to keep us stuck in the status quo.

Steven Pressfield, in his book *Do the Work*, describes the resistance that our lizard brain puts up like this: "If you've got a head, you've got a voice of Resistance inside it. The enemy is in you, but it is not you. No moral judgment attaches to the possession of it. You "have" Resistance the same way you "have" a heartbeat. You are blameless. You retain free will and the capacity to act."

"Free will and the capacity to act"—that's what we've got. Regardless of how today or the day before or the day before that went, we still have a choice today, right now.

A friend of mine compared doing this work to running a marathon. You set your sights on completing the marathon, but the real work is making the choice—every week, every day, every moment—to practice and train and do your very best.

Our challenge is to do the work, to *choose* to show up as our *best* self, every day.

* * *

Exercising the will to *Extend* ourselves on behalf of others is the foundation of great leadership. It is a daily, moment-by-moment choice. Sometimes we're brilliant at it and sometimes we're less than brilliant. We accept that it's a practice and we make the effort every day.

CONCLUSION

We're not here to make a difference. We're here to *be* a difference.

I hope, after reading this book, that you feel like you really do have time to lead. I hope you're entertaining the idea that leading isn't something you *do*; it's someone you are.

And I hope that that idea gives you both a sense of relief and a very real sense of responsibility.

If you believe that leadership is someone you are, not something you do, then you will know that you are *always* leading. Every time you walk into a room, every time you interact with someone, every time you make a decision, you are leading. That means it's not about *making* time to lead, it's about choosing how you want to show up in every interaction, in everything you do, so that the leadership you're providing is what you want it to be.

This perspective of leadership doesn't require you to *make* time for leadership, because you know that you are leading in everything you do. Finding time to lead in this way requires you to shift from doing to being. It asks that you *Embark* on a never-ending journey toward becoming the leader you aspire to be. It pushes you to *Explore* your personal story and to be true to yourself while also recognizing and sharing the default modes that keep you from being your *best* self.

Shifting your perspective from doing to being changes how you show up. It doesn't mean that you don't do things. It means that you believe that leadership is about how you *choose* to *be*. You recognize that how you show up may actually be the most important part of what you do.

I hope that you have a sense now of how to choose who you want to be. Leadership demands a lot of us, and we need to be ever vigilant so that we are ready to heed its call. You are a hero on a hero's journey, and this is your epic tale. Confront the challenges as well as you can. Ultimately, we are measured not by what we get done, but by who we are.

I hope you've reached the end of this book with a sense of why understanding is important, and why it is often more important than knowing. The shift from knowing to understanding is one that can be challenging for us high-achieving types. We like to *know*. And we feel like others expect us to know (and sometimes they're right to expect that).

Our very human brains are wired for knowing, for certainty. When we can know and predict, we are more assured of success. We don't have to face the unknown. We don't have to entertain the possibility of failure.

And yet, if we are going to lead, we need to be prepared to learn—from every success and every failure. We need to *Expand* our thinking to embrace the paradoxes that are inherent in growth. Rather than approaching things as either/or, black and white, we can understand that two things can *both* be true. With that understanding, we can then hold space for "what if," so that creative solutions can emerge.

Understanding also requires us to *Engage*. We are, each of us, unique individuals who bring our own stories and life experiences and points of view to every situation, conversation, decision, and action. When we come together, as we obviously must when work needs to get done in concert with each other, we bring our unique selves into a social system. We influence that system at the same time the system influences us.

"Business is a human enterprise. It may even be why we call a business a 'company'—because it is a collection of people in the company of other people. It's the company that matters."
~ Simon Sinek, *Leaders Eat Last*

In the shift from knowing to understanding, we come to see that engaging with others in productive and meaningful ways is the essence of our work. We recognize that leadership is not merely something *we* do; it is happening all the time, often without us. We help people find meaning and we support them with the narratives that give them the courage to be the kind of leader *they* want to be.

And, finally, I hope that you are embracing the shift from reacting to responding. Our reactions are often the result of our own personal point of view, and they are dramatically influenced by our lizard brain warning us of potential dangers. When we shift from reacting to responding, we're better able to consider our responses and *choose* how we want to show up.

When we're responding instead of reacting, we're able to shift our perspective and think of ourselves as the mentor instead of thinking of ourselves only as the hero. From the perspective of mentor, we *Encourage* those around us. We train ourselves to glimpse greatness and to invite it into the room. The Mentor becomes our starring role. We act on behalf of the hero, and telling the truth becomes our natural response.

I hope you are committed to *Evolve*, eager to push yourself to your own edges and into the space of the unknown where true growth happens. I hope you can see yourself patiently moving through the challenges that present themselves in the unknown, allowing time and space for the best way forward to emerge. And I hope you can see yourself holding space for others as you lead them into the unknown, so that they arrive with you on the other side, ready to take the next big leap.

And, finally, I challenge you to *Extend* yourself. Every day. I hope these practices help you find the will to extend yourself on behalf of others, and that you are inspired to celebrate the human connection that unleashes our potential, individually and collectively.

* * *

There is greatness in you. Put it out there in the world in ways that make a positive difference—for you, for your company, for the people who come to work with and for you, for your family, your community, your industry, our country, and our world.

You have a great opportunity.

Make the most of it.

FURTHER READING

I'm grateful to the amazing thinkers and authors who have influenced my own thinking on this topic over the last three decades. May you find their books and offerings as inspirational and thought-provoking as I have.

BOOKS

Simon Sinek, *Start with Why* and *Leaders Eat Last*

Seth Godin, *The Icarus Deception*

Peter Block, *The Answer to How is Yes* and *Community: The Sense of Belonging*

Carol Dweck, *Mindset*

Margaret Wheatley, *Leadership and the New Science*

Chogyam Trungpa, *Shambhala: The Sacred Path of the Warrior*

Kimberly Schneider, *Everything You Need is Right Here*

Margaret Wheatley and Deborah Friese, *Walk Out Walk On*

Brené Brown, *Daring Greatly*

Cynthia Bourgeault, *The Holy Trinity and the Law of Three*

Henri Nouwen, *Reaching Out* and *Spiritual Direction*

Daniel Goleman, *Emotional Intelligence*

Scott Peck, *The Road Less Traveled*

Robert Grudin, *Time and the Art of Living*

Peter Senge, *The Fifth Discipline*

David Hutchens, *Circle of the 9 Muses*

John Medina, *Brain Rules*

Jim Collins, *Good to Great*

Stephen Pressfield, *Do the Work*

Bob Chapman and Raj Sisodia, *Everybody Matters*

Sarah Lewis, *The Rise*

Patrick Lenioni, *The Advantage*

Parker Palmer, *A Hidden Wholeness*

LINKS

Krista Tippett and her show, *On Being:* http://www.onbeing.org/

Maria Popova and the Sunday morning delight that is *Brain Pickings:* https://www.brainpickings.org/

Seth Godin: http://www.sethgodin.com

Kimberly Schneider: *http://www.Kimberly. Schneider.com*

BW Leadership Institute: http://bwleadershipinstitute.com/

Cognitive Edge: http://cognitive-edge.com/

Chris Corrigan: http://www.chriscorrigan.com/parkinglot/

Art of Hosting: http://www.artofhosting.org/

Margaret Wheatley: http://margaretwheatley.com/

Brené Brown: http://brenebrown.com/

Simon Sinek: https://www.startwithwhy.com/

Tuesday Ryan-Hart: http://www.tuesdayryanhart.com/

ARTICLES

"Making Common Sense—Leadership as Meaning-Making in a Community of Practice" by Wilfred H. Drath and Charles J. Palus (Center for Creative Leadership, 1994). http://www.leadingeffectively.com/interdependent-leadership/wp-content/uploads/2012/10/Making-Common-Sense-Drath-and-Palus-1994.pdf

"A Leader's Framework for Decision Making," by David J. Snowden and Mary E. Boone (Harvard Business Review, November, 2007). https://hbr.org/2007/11/a-leaders-framework-for-decision-making

"How Great Companies Think Differently" by Rosabeth Moss Kanter (Harvard Business Review, November, 2011). https://hbr.org/2011/11/how-great-companies-think-differently

"Can One Man Save American Business?" by Dorian Rolston (Psychology Today, July, 2013). https://www.psychologytoday.com/articles/201307/can-one-man-save-american-business

"The Top 22 Mistakes of First-Time CEOs" by Edwin Miller (Venture Beat, August, 2014). http://venturebeat.com/2014/08/04/the-top-22-mistakes-of-first-time-ceos/

VIDEOS

Brené Brown: "The Power of Vulnerability" (TEDxHouston, June, 2010). https://www.ted.com/talks/brene_brown_on_vulnerability?language=en

Simon Sinek: "How Great Leaders Inspire Action" (TEDxPuget Sound, September, 2009). (https://www.ted.com/talks/simon_sinek_how_great_leaders_inspire_action?language=en)

Simon Sinek: "Why Good Leaders Make You Feel Safe" (TED, March, 2014). https://www.ted.com/talks/simon_sinek_why_good_leaders_make_you_feel_safe

Kim Scott: "Radical Candor—The Surprising Secret to Being a Good Boss" (First Round Review, December 2015). http://www.kimmalonescott.com/

ACKNOWLEDGMENTS

The only logical place for me to start in a list of acknowledgments is to express my profound gratitude to "the gang"—John, Danny, David, Stuart, Gay, and Lisa. Thank you for always truly seeing me. I'm ever so grateful to each of you for helping me keep my head about me for 35 years (and counting) and for always remembering the words to my song, even when I've forgotten them. (With a heap of extra gratitude to John, who keeps the vampires at bay.)

Thanks to the GLAD Team that brings me so much joy. To my husband, Dan, who inspires me with his capacity for listening and profound acceptance. To my stepson, Aidan, whose view of the world teaches me new things every day. And to Grace, my wise and creative daughter. Being your mom is, without a doubt, the most wonderful job I'll ever have.

Thanks to my dad, who was always perfectly himself in the most comforting ways. I miss you. And thanks to my mom, who has always been completely and utterly supportive of me, in spite of the fact that I've never had a job that she can explain to her friends.

Many of the ideas and concepts in this book came to life in my work with Zack Boyers. I am forever grateful for your partnership and friendship. I'm honored by the incredible trust you placed in me and for your belief in the crazy ideas that get hatched in my head. It has truly been one of the profound honors of my life to have played a role in helping you build the company (and the world) you imagine.

I am thrilled to be able to work with my tremendous team of colleagues and friends at Elements Partnership. I'm grateful to Lindsay, for her intense belief in me and for the love and support she provides (to me and my whole family); to Jami, for her warmth and extrovert energy, for the laughs and for *always* being there; to John, for being the manager balance to my artist self and for pushing me to do all kinds of important things (like write this book); and to Catherine, who I've wanted to hire since she was twelve years old and whose contributions are just starting to be felt. I'm grateful for each one of you and am so very proud of the good work we're able to do together.

I'm grateful for many hours spent over tea and orange scones with Kimberly Schneider, sharing ideas and insights and co-creating important work. Our conversations and connections are reflected in these pages.

I would be remiss if I didn't thank Tom Hoerr, who hired me—when I was 21 years old—to create something important and meaningful, and who still calls himself my "first and only boss." Thank you for considering mentoring me one of your most important jobs.

Thanks to Jim McLeod, who taught me, by his example, that all greatness comes from goodness. I feel your presence in so many lovely ways.

Thanks to Dr. Angela Lauria of the Author Incubator, who literally said things to me like (in this order): "I had trouble staying awake for this bullshit sentence" and "This may be some of the best flap copy I've ever read," "This is such a mess you need to start over" and "This is not a college paper. I want to know what *you* think." You authentically model believing in people before they believe in themselves, and you always come from place of love. Thanks for helping me get out of my own way.

Much gratitude to my Managing Editor, Grace Kerina. Your patience, knowledge and steady hand made this a better book and made me a better author.

My heartfelt thanks to Chris Corrigan, Caitlin Frost, Tuesday Ryan-Hart, and everyone who contributes to the Art of Hosting movement. Your insights and generosity have expanded my thinking and inspired me to think more deeply about my own practice.

Over the last 30 years, I have had the privilege of working with many, many extraordinary people and organizations too numerous to mention. Whether it was designing and facilitating meetings, providing training, creating strategic plans, partnering over the course of many years, navigating through change and crisis, starting new organizations, providing coaching and mentoring, or just sitting quietly together in the tough times, it has been my great privilege to be part of your journeys, and I'm proud of any small contributions I've made to your incredible work. Thank you for *all* that you have taught me.

I'm thankful for *so* many people who have shared this journey with me and who have helped to bring my best self forward into the world. I am humbled by your belief in me and ever so grateful to be sharing this time and space with you.

ABOUT THE AUTHOR

Leslie Peters is the Founder, CEO, and Chief Facilitator at Elements Partnership, a consulting practice that helps people and organizations get unstuck.

Leslie launched Elements Partnership in 2011 with one simple belief: that people are hungry for *real* conversation.

The team at Elements Partnership provides dynamic, interactive learning experiences that shift perspectives, build relationships, and create new behaviors.

Over the last 25 years, Leslie has provided counsel and training in organizational development, strategic planning, and leadership development to for-profit and non-profit organizations across the country.

Leslie has a bachelor's degree in English and an MBA from Washington University in St. Louis. She cares deeply about engagement, leadership, and the kinds of shared experiences that lead to real change in individuals, groups, and organizations.

She's married to a remarkable musician and composer named Dan Rubright and she has a daughter, Grace, and a stepson, Aidan. Together, they call themselves the GLAD Team (**G**race, **L**eslie, **A**idan, and **D**an).

Website: www.FindingTimeToLead.com and www.elementspartnership.com

Blog: www.elementspartnership.com/unwound/

Email: info@findingtimetolead.com

Facebook: @elementspartnership (www.facebook.com/elementspartnership/)

LinkedIn: @Elements Partnership (www.linkedin.com/company/6606915)

difference press

Difference Press offers entrepreneurs, including life coaches, healers, consultants, and community leaders, a comprehensive solution to get their books written, published, and promoted. A boutique-style alternative to self-publishing, Difference Press boasts a fair and easy-to-understand profit structure, low-priced author copies, and author-friendly contract terms. Its founder, Dr. Angela Lauria, has been bringing to life the literary ventures of hundreds of authors-in-transformation since 1994.

LET'S MAKE A DIFFERENCE WITH YOUR BOOK

You've seen other people make a difference with a book. Now it's your turn. If you are ready to stop watching and start taking massive action, reach out.

"Yes, I'm ready!"

In a market where hundreds of thousands books are published every year and are never heard from again, all participants of The Author Incubator have bestsellers that are actively changing lives and making a difference.

In two years we've created over 134 bestselling books in a row, 90% from first-time authors. We do this by selecting the highest quality and highest potential applicants for our future programs.

Our program doesn't just teach you how to write a book—our team of coaches, developmental editors, copy editors, art directors, and marketing experts incubate you from book idea to published bestseller, ensuring that the book you create can actually make a difference in the world. Then we give you the training you need to use your book to make the difference you want to make in the world, or to create a business out of serving your readers. If you have life-or world-changing ideas or services, a servant's heart, and the willingness to do what it REALLY takes to make a difference in the world with your book, go to http://theauthorincubator.com/apply/ to complete an application for the program today.

OTHER BOOKS BY DIFFERENCE PRESS

*Lasting Love
At Last: The
Gay Guide To
Attracting the
Relationship of
Your Dreams*

by Amari Ice

*...But I'm Not
Racist!: Tools for
Well-Meaning
Whites*

by Kathy Obear

*Who the Fuck Am I
To Be a Coach:
A Warrior's Guide
to Building a
Wildly Successful
Coaching Business
From the Inside
Out*

by Megan Jo Wilson

*Your Key to the
Akashic Records:
Fulfill Your Soul's
Highest Potential*

by Jiayuh Chyan

*Standing Up: From
Renegade Professor
to Middle-Aged
Comic*

by Ada Cheng

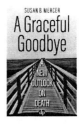

*A Graceful
Goodbye: A New
Outlook on Death*

by Susan B. Mercer

THANK YOU

You can download a free copy of the **Finding Time to Lead Tool Kit** from our website: FindingTimeToLead.com. The Kit includes the materials I reference in the book, plus a few bonus materials including additional worksheets, links, and downloads.

While you're on the website, you can sign up to receive the **free audio series** we created to support you as you *Embark* on your own personal leadership journey.

Making and sustaining the three shifts is an ongoing practice. If you're interested in personalized training for you or your team as you pursue your journey toward great leadership, you can inquire at FindingTimeToLead.com or email us at info@findingtimetolead.com. We look forward to talking with you!

CPSIA information can be obtained
at www.ICGtesting.com
Printed in the USA
FFOW04n0612101217
43964082-43087FF